Witness To The Las … aj

Witness to the
Last Years of The Raj

Ronald Perkin

Librario

Published by

Librario Publishing Ltd.

ISBN 10 : 1-904440-88-6
ISBN 13 : 978-1904440888

Copies can be ordered from retail
or via the internet at:
www.librario.com

or from:

Brough House
Milton Brodie
Kinloss
Moray
IV36 2UA
Tel / Fax: 01343 850178

Printed in Times.

Cover design and layout by Steven James
www.chimeracreations.co.uk

Printed and bound by
4edge Ltd, Hockley. www.4edge.co.uk

CONTENTS

Chapter 1 : 1919 – 1939

Childhood, Schooldays, RMC Sandhurst

My grandparents (on my father's side) were both graduates from the Royal College of Art, Kensington. My grandfather was a fine artist and draftsman. He went on to found two educational institutions in Tiverton, Devon, where he was also the art master at Blundells School. My grandmother was in the first term/batch of women ever to get a degree. She was, in our opinion, an even better artist, and also a wood carver in her own right. Although she never went professional she was an ARA and her pictures were often hung in the Royal Academy. None of their pictures, and there are many, have been sold. They are all distributed throughout the family, where they are retained with great pride. I myself have most of her carvings. They had two sons and a daughter. My father, the eldest, on leaving Blundells School (one of the oldest schools in England), went out to India and joined the Indian Police in November 1909. His brother was killed on the first day of the Battle of the Somme – 1st July 1911 – the day on which the British Army suffered more casualties than before, or at any time since i.e. 20,000 killed and double that number wounded.

My parents had four children, all born in India. Three were born in Shillong, Assam where my maternal grandparents lived and one, myself, in Dhanbad, Bihar. It was the normal practice in those far off days of Empire for officers of the Colonial Services to send their children back to England for their education. In our family we were no exception. My eldest sister (Peggy) was left with our father's parents in Oxford at three years of age. My brother (Kenneth) and I followed in 1925 when I was 5 years old and the youngest sister Beryl was brought back some years later, in 1930 I think it was. My brother and I were left with the family of McMichaels – who were our guardians from then on. Mr McMichael had been at school with my father and was maths master at St Edward's School, Oxford.

We stayed with this family for many years; I personally was with them until I left to join the Indian Army in 1939 – after some 15 happy years.

The McMichaels were a very nice couple but one thing that they lacked was any overt TLC (tender loving care). I don't recall ever getting hugs or kisses from the age of 5 onwards. I will digress here to record that when I was about 11 years of age, I and another boy were admitted to our school (St Edward's) sanatorium and operating theatre to have our tonsils out. I had it done first and when I was still muzzy from the anaesthetic I asked the ward nurse how the other boy was doing, whereupon she bent over and kissed me. I still remember this incident even though it happened over seventy years ago! When our parents did come back we were really past expecting anything like that. We had our paternal grandparents living nearby in Oxford but they were rather too old for us and they were also typically Victorian in their outlook. She was never allowed to go out shopping by herself nor was she permitted to put on the "wireless"! One day they were both out in the front garden when the vicar came along and stopped to talk to them over the front gate, whereupon my grandfather told my grandmother to "go indoors, Lily"! My sisters attended the academically excellent Girls' High School in Oxford; however it was not a boarding school as such, although there was a lady near the school who took in girls, such as my sisters, during the term time. In the holidays they were farmed out to relations or stayed with school friends. They did not have the same stable base that my brother and I had with the McMichaels, in that we always knew where we would be in the holidays. On most Sundays, throughout the year, we four children would foregather at our grandparents for tea and sometimes lunch – where we were very well fed!

At that time the McMichaels had two sons, (Bill and Michael) and a daughter (Cicely); later there was another daughter, Mary. I really knew them far better than my own parents. In those first 15 years of my life our parents didn't often come back on leave to England. Also in those days there was no such thing as air travel, very limited telephonic communication and ship journeys (which carried the Royal Mail) took at least three weeks to and from India. If I was ill, and my parents informed (by sea mail), they would not hear about it for three weeks, then six weeks later I would get a letter back from my mother saying that she hoped I was feeling better! Colonial officers were only granted long leave back to England every 3 or 4 years. In our case they didn't come back the first time for five years – when I was 11 years old. We got used to it and very thankfully, we were happy with our "guardians".

Our parents were very regular letter writers and we received a letter from both of them every week without fail. Later on in life I met other boys in similar circumstances and none of them was happy with his adopted parents.

Apart from my brother and I, the McMichaels took in other boys now and again, mostly brothers and from St Edwards as well. Of the three sets of brothers (one pair were the Gibsons: the youngest one Guy, was the famous 'Dam' Buster), Mr McMichael liked to recount that of the boys he had 'fathered', between them they had earned the following medals in the 1939/45 War, one VC, three DFCs, two DSOs, one Croix de Guerre, four MCs and my brother, a pilot in the Photographic Unit flying unarmed aircraft, was shot down twice over Burma but lived to survive the War.

In 1929 my brother and I were sent to Magdalen College School, Oxford. There, a lot of extremely nasty bullying was allowed to exist. We were not bullied at all, perhaps because we were too small, but I think it was for another reason. Our father, I have always supposed, deemed it advisable for us to learn to box and so be able to look after ourselves in his absence. So he arranged that, three times a week, we would walk down to the Oxford University gymnasium and take boxing lessons with the University coach who, incidentally, was one of the last bare fist boxers of his day. In fact we were too small to take on the bullyboys but I have always thought that they did not quite know how much (or how little!) we knew about boxing and therefore left us alone!

In 1931, through some back door juggling by Mr McMichael, my brother and I were accepted to St Edward's School without having to take the common entrance exam and further, we were both under the normal age of entrance, he was 13 and I was 11, three years younger than normal. I would not recommend this and I think that it did not help me in my studies – quite the contrary.

St Edward's School, in 1939, was a comparatively small public school with a total of about 360 boys – but now, in 2004, it has increased very considerably to over 600, and of course it is now co-educational. Small though it was by many other public school standards, nevertheless, it sent a greater per cent of its Old Boys to fight in the Boer War and First War than most other public schools.

And in the Second War it was more or less the same thing. During the period of 1939–45 over 120 of the Old Boys were killed serving their country – a very large proportion. Furthermore the list of its medal tally is quite astonishing. One VC; one GC; 13 DSOs; 28 DFCs; 29 MC; 2MMs; 7 DSCs; plus MBEs , OBEs and BEMs and several had foreign decorations eg; 'No legs'– Douglas Bader; Guy ('dambuster') Gibson and Adrian 'Warby' Warburton and others. The RAF seemed to draw more than its fair share of heroes from the school, so much so that the Air Council presented the Chapel with a window inscribed with the words: "To mark the fine record of the boys from this school in the Royal Air Force".

Although there was little or no bullying by boys at this school I, myself experienced quite a lot, for a number of years, just from one particular master whose French and science classes I had to endure. He obviously took a dislike to me and though he may have had some cause, in that I was by no means a star pupil – indeed I must have appeared to him to be reluctant to learn anything he had to impart, nevertheless I was only 12 or 13 years old. On one occasion he threw all my books out of the third floor window, on another he made me stand on my head on the hard wooden floor and another he made me push my nose right down into a jar of strong-smelling chlorine but worst of all he kept on giving me extra drills and detentions, which were held on half-holidays. My guardian (Mr McMichael) got to hear of this (not from me) and it was stopped.

Although I was not an academic by any stretch of imagination I did manage to pass the required school certificate exams. I was, however, very interested in playing games! During my time at St Edwards (I was there for 7 years) I won every swimming and diving cup in all three categories, junior, colt and senior. I also acquired the dubious distinction of holding the record for beatings – three of which I well recall were entirely undeserved. I really don't think that they did me any harm – in fact they made me somewhat stoical and phlegmatic – both of which characteristics stood me in good stead in the War years to follow. I don't hold any strong views about corporal punishment but I very much doubt whether its application does any lasting harm to most children – in my case it did not act as a deterrent! One point I would make here is that when I rose to become a Senior Prefect, I would not apply the rod myself but passed on the duty to others. I didn't like the action of hitting another boy without him being allowed to hit back at me.

I was captain of boxing, got my athletics colours, and was in the gymnastics team and swimming teams. I was also captain of the 2nd XV rugger team for two years but never got into the 1st XV, although I often played for it. The rugger master in charge and I did not get on well!

Whilst at school I decided to join the Army so I left school in December 1937 and went on to the Royal Military College, Sandhurst in January 1938. All my contemporaries went up to Oxford or Cambridge but I had no ambitions in that direction – too academic for my liking! However, I had many invitations to their college dinners, which were most enjoyable, if not too much so!

In those days Sandhurst was very much a fee-paying institution and all uniforms, boots, sword, food etc. were not issued but had to be purchased (by one's parents, of course). Having passed the required exam and at my father's instigation, I applied for a King's India Cadetship which would earn some financial relief for my father. The Sandhurst fee used to be about £500 for the 18 months' course of three terms, quite a large sum in those pre-war days. When I went into the interview room I was confronted by a board of some six senior officers – all of whom seemed to be coughing!

After the preliminary introduction I was asked one question which I really should have prepared myself for, but hadn't. The question was: "Why do you want to go into the Indian Army?" As I had not prepared myself for this I merely said that I did not like the climate in England. This seemed to amuse the board and after the laughter and coughing had subsided I left the room. I don't recall anything else being asked or said to me.

Some weeks later the result of this interview was announced – I had passed and been granted the Cadetship, so saving my father £150! The more practical result was that I was then earmarked for the Indian Army. To get into the Indian Army was the ambition of most cadets (not least because the pay was greater than in the British Army) and one had to 'pass out' fairly high up – so this was one hurdle I was now excused.

I did not distinguish myself at Sandhurst – not academically anyway, but I did get my 'blues' for boxing and swimming and was also in the gymnastics' display team. I 'passed out' of Sandhurst in July 1939, and was commissioned (2nd Lieutenant) on 1st July that year in the ULIA (Unattached List of the Indian Army).

Now might a good a time as any to outline what the life of a Sandhurst GC "gentleman cadet" was like in the 1930s and how the 18 months shaped my particular life.

The day after we arrived, in our usual civilian clothes, we were marched everywhere at the quick pace of the Rifle Brigades. Not being used to this we all suffered stiffness of the calf muscles; however this passed off. Then, over the following weeks, we received our various regulation uniforms which included the following items:

Normal drill parade uniform with, cap boots and puttees; Ceremonial dress uniform, cap, boots and puttees; PT (physical training) kit consisting of white trousers, shorts and T shirt; red and white striped blazer and, not forgetting, a red and white striped 'pill box' hat; equestrian uniform including riding breeches, leather calf length gaiters; Evening 'blues' high-necked dress uniform for dinner; Canvas overalls for wearing on the rifle range and finally sports kit depending on what sport(s) one took part in. So – in the course of a day the uniform would be changed at least four times – generally more.

Our first nine weeks were spent, very largely, on the 'square' being drilled up and down and backwards and forwards by our CSM (Company Sergeant Major) – a seconded NCO from one of the Guards regiments. They were extremely good at their jobs and ranted and raved at us until we got everything right. Even though they were far from polite they would always finish up with a "Sir" e.g. "You are a bone idle detail Mr Perkin – SIR." They would call us Mister and we called them "staff" – except the RSM whom we had to call "Sir" and he would call us "sir" back again.

Until we had come off the 'square' (after 9 weeks) we could not leave the Sandhurst grounds. We were allocated a batman between 5 or 6 cadets and he would keep our boots, belts and room clean. But we had to polish our own ceremonial dress boots, chin strap for our dress cap, and look after our rifles and, most important of all, our own bayonet scabbard. At the end of 9 weeks the company SUO (Senior Under Officer – a cadet) would inspect each item and if satisfied one could then apply for weekend leaves and go out of the Sandhurst grounds into Camberley, Farnborough or Aldershot. But it was pretty well known that, on principle, there would always be something wrong to delay this 'freedom'.

There were, in those days, four companies of about 100 cadets each, Nos. 1, 3, 4 and and 5 . . . I believe that No. 2 had been disbanded many years before owing to some misdemeanour. Each company was divided into three sections, The first term cadets comprised the Junior section; the Intermediate section the second term cadets, some of whom would be granted a temporary cadet rank and finally the Seniors of whom some were promoted to Cadet Sergeants; JUOs (Junior Under Officer) of platoon and SUOs (Senior Under Officer) of their company. Of the four companies one of the SUOs would be granted the Sword of Honour – on the final Passing Out Parade.

1 and 3 Companies were situated in the New Buildings with 4 and 5 in the old Buildings. Each building had what was called a FGS (Fancy Goods Store) which, when it was open, served various beverages including beer, cigarettes and some snacks. One would sign a 'chit' for purchases. It was the normal practice that the parents of each cadet would provide him with £3 a month pocket money which would be credited to his account. Woe betide any cadet if he ever got overdrawn – even by 1d. I don't know if any cadet was allowed to have more then the £3 no matter how wealthy the parents might be. By the end of the month everyone was absolutely skint. In my case, my parents being overseas, I was given my allocation for 3 months at a time so at the beginning of each quarter I always had two months in hand compared to the others. This state of my affluence soon got around and I became a banker – albeit a very temporary one. I would be asked to lend money until the next pay-in day.

Each company was commanded by a regular Regimental major and four captains. These also had teaching duties. Additionally there were the CSM and four other NCOs. Each company had an anteroom where one could sit and read papers and there was also a billiard table. We would congregate in this room before going into to dinner when there was also a roll call. We had formal dinners five nights a week when four or five courses were served up by the menservants.

Apart from drills, PT, riding, range practice and games we had a certain number of academic lessons – not too many! and these were held in the various *Halls of Study*. The lessons were mostly applicable to military matters e.g. military history, army formations, staff duties, vehicle maintenance, etc.

On Sundays there would be a full Church Parade. The majority of cadets were C. of E. (Church of England). After the parade we would be marched off to the RMC chapel but the RC (Roman Catholic) contingent would go to the RC chapel, while the rest of other denominations would just fall out.

Discipline was strict but the punishments not severe – such as being confined to the Sandhurst grounds. I recall one incidence when we were told to address an envelope to our parents – using capital letters. I forgot and wrote in freehand small case for which offence I was confined to the grounds for three weeks. On another occasion a cadet went up to London for some reason or other but his return journey was delayed many hours on account of thick fog condtions. He was told this was not a valid excuse as he should have checked on the weather forecast before setting out! He was gated for the rest of the term. We always had to be back in our rooms by 11p.m. unless we had obtained a special pass. No girls were allowed on the premises 'at all – at all' as the Irish would say. Once every term there would be a dance. These were held in the gymnasium and were very colourful affairs as full dress uniforms were worn by all officers and these varied very much from regiment to regiment – particularly those of the Indian Army. In the summer term was held the famous June Ball. There were three bands – one down by the lakes where a dance floor would be erected and the trees around the lake illuminated. There were long queues for the flat bottomed boats!

For these dances there was always a problem in finding accommodation in and around Sandhurst for the girls. I had invited a girl (Cicely McMichael) and got a room for her at the Black Horse Inn in Blackwater, however two other girls failed to get a room anywhere so I pushed them in with my partner – three to a bed!

Whilst at Sandhurst, during our second term, we cadets applied for regiments we hoped would accept us. The various regiments would send down senior officers to conduct interviews of the hopefuls – in many instances, of course, the selection had already been made as some cadets had family and other ties. To get into the Guards, or some cavalry regiments, for instance, one would have to have quite a large private income to be considered at all! Those of us who were destined for the Indian Army regiments were initially posted to a British Regiment in India – to what was known as the ULIA (Unattached List of the Indian Army). This was because, in the Indian regiments one got great responsibility almost straight away, whereas a subaltern in a British regiment might serve for many years before he was trusted to any responsible appointment, so we had to learn how to be junior officers first! This attachment was for the duration of one year after which you joined your Indian regiment. I, and five officers from Sandhurst plus two Indian Officers from Dehru Dun – the equivalent Indian Military College, were posted to the Royal Inniskilling Fusiliers, which was stationed up in a very enviable hill station in Southern India, at Wellington in the Nilgiri Hills – 6000 ft up. (In passing I would point out that this regiment was one of the more wealthy ones in that most of the officers, if not all, had some private income to eke out army salaries.)

Before leaving the UK, (I didn't know for how many years) I thought I would go and visit various friends and relatives. The first was my brother who was, at that time, a flying instructor at Marshall's aerodrome outside Cambridge. There he took me up in a Tiger Moth, a single-engine training biplane. This plane had a wooden framework, covered in a sort of cellulose. The pilot was in the front seat and the passenger, me, in the back. I was then subjected to every aerobatic trick known to my brother, looping the loop, flying upside down, etc. and worst of all the 'falling leaf'.

The next visit I remember was to Hendon airfield (or it might have been North Holt) where my friend Guy Gibson was serving. This was an RAF station alongside of which ran a main road. The public used to stop their cars, get out and watch the aircraft taking off and landing. The pilots used to come down very, very low over these parked cars just to scare the spectators, but unfortunately Guy rather overdid this and took the top off one of the cars and while I was there he was awaiting the outcome of a Court of Inquiry into this 'accident'. After lunch, about ten of the pilots (myself and Guy included) went into the anteroom and there drank rather a lot of liquor. Someone suggested we try to see how many drawing pins we could drive into our forearms – and we did, very many. I was not too keen on this pastime and even less so when they upped the drawing pins to full sized pins but, being the only army officer present I could hardly back out! Before condemning this as a mindless frolic one must remember all these young men, the following year, became Battle of Britain pilots and everybody knows what they could, and did do, for their country.

A month after we were commissioned I was on board the Troopship *Nevassa* bound for India. There were 118 of us just out of Sandhurst going out to join either the Indian Army or British Regiments. I don't recall how many BORs (British Other Ranks) there were also on board but I do remember that three army nurses (QAIMNS) accompanied us. Without meaning to be rude I must admit that they were NOT adjudged beauties and were nicknamed FAITH, HOPE and CHARITY, but be that as it may, by the time we got to Suez and without other female company, they were in great demand at the first dance held on board!

In those days of course, there was no such thing as air conditioning and the trip was carried out during the hottest time of the year (August). At night we had to wear full evening uniform. It was so hot in the Red Sea, as there was a following wind, that the ship was turned round for a few hours, night and day, to catch and suck the wind down into the ship's lower decks. We officers (about 120 in all), each shared a cabin between two, while the troops were billeted down below in hammocks in the stifling heat – as far as I am aware they all survived the journey. I recall, while officiating as Officer-of-the-day, having to go the rounds of the ship to visit the various sentry posts at specified points (e.g. fire extinguisher point). These sentries had to be in uniform, albeit khaki drill, but had to wear the large solar topis, even though they were positioned down in the depths of the ship where no air or light penetrated! The journey took just over three weeks to get to Bombay. In transit we (the officers), were allowed ashore only once for a few hours at Port Said, where we all made the obligatory visit to the famous shop, Simon Artz.

Chapter 2 : 1939

Sea Journey to India, Joining Inniskilling Fusiliers (ULIA)

The three-week sea journey was completed in mid-August and we were met at Bombay (now called Mumbai) by the forwarding military authorities who sent us off on our respective train journeys to our final destinations. On our train were the four of us from the RMC plus a senior captain of the Inniskillings. We four were allocated a four-berth compartment and the captain a two-berth one. Compartments had two or four beds and a toilet/WC en suite. No air conditioning of course, but there were ceiling fans, so it was the practice to order a tin tub in which was placed a block of ice weighing 80lb (approx.), then one would focus the fans onto this tub of ice thereby distributing the cool air around the compartment. This ice would keep the temperature down by about 10 degrees and would last about 8 hours so we would pass the message down the line to have a replacement block delivered at the required station. As with air conditioning nowadays, the windows would be kept shut to prevent the very hot air outside coming in. First Class passengers would order food at the stations from the railway restaurant contractors and it would then be brought on board at some agreed forward station. There were no restaurant carriages in those days.

On the second day of the journey, when we arrived at a station, I heard my name being called out by someone on the platform, presumably the stationmaster. He then came up to inform me that a special carriage had been attached to the train for my onward passage. This was a great boon as it gave us much more room and comfort, due to the presence of chairs etc. that had been lacking in the compartment. On further questioning it turned out that this facility had been organized by a distant cousin of mine who held some senior post in the Indian Railway system of Southern India where he was based in Madras. I never did find out how he came to know (a) that I had arrived in India and (b) which train I was travelling on. I had only met him once some years before while he was back in England on leave. On reaching Madras we changed trains and headed for Wellington, which military station is situated to the West of Madras 6000ft up in the Nilgiri Hills. (It was renowned for being one of the best military stations in India.) The last leg of the journey takes the best part of a day and starts at a station called Mettapolyam from where a ratchet-type engine pulls the carriages up the very steep mountain to Wellington where the Inniskillings were stationed. There is a motor road going up and is reputed to have 33 hairpin bends with lots of sheer drops over the side, should one be unfortunate enough to misjudge one's corners!

The Inniskilling barracks were very much on the lines of the standard pattern throughout the East: high ceilings, plenty of room with dormitories for the troops housing about 18 – 20 soldiers to each room. We bachelor officers were allotted to a 'chummery' – a building on two floors with four rooms up and down. There were seven of us in this one and we each had a large room with a bathroom/wc en suite. This bathroom contained a galvanised tin tub for a bath, a washbasin on a metal tripod, and a 'thunderbox' loo seat with a bucket underneath. There was no running water of course, nor flush toilet. The bucket would be emptied periodically by the 'sweeper', and water provided by our bearers in a tin jug. The furniture in each room was standardized (throughout India). A bed (single), an upright chair, a dressing table and mirror, a feet-up wicker chair and a ceiling fan which was left running all the time. We all paid the standard furniture rental (to a contractor) wherever we might be stationed. Married quarters were also standard but included a few more items. One could, of course, buy other pieces as personal property.

The next day after our arrival – the news got around very quickly – men began to arrive offering their services as bearers and from them we made our respective choices. No sooner had we selected one than he would produce a young lad to be his assistant/learner, who then became our 'chokra'. In addition to these two between us, we hired a sweeper who did the 'honours' to our bathroom/wc and also a Mali to tend the garden and fetch water for our baths.

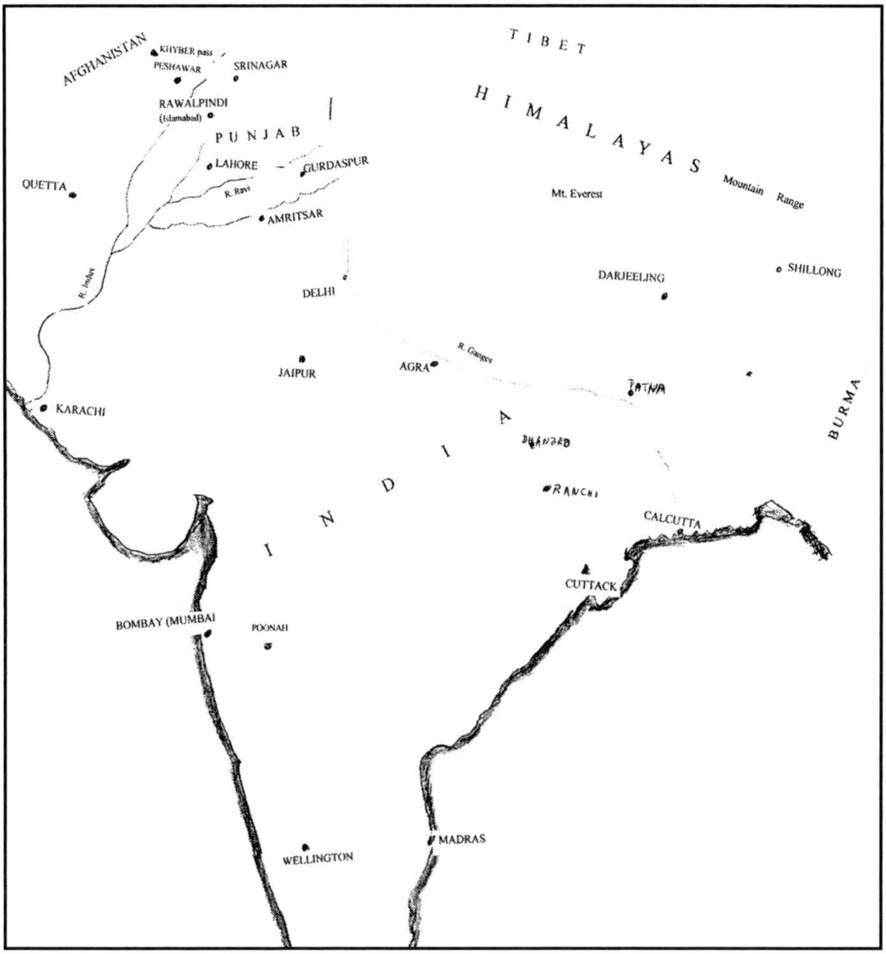

Map of India

In passing, I would mention that I took up golf in Wellington and so employed a full time caddy and he in turn took on an assistant (age wallah) whose main preoccupation, when I was playing, was to keep an eye on the ball and see that it didn't get lost or picked up by crows. I suppose that I paid them about £1 per month. My bearer got the standard Indian Army pay for bearers, which was about £3 plus £1 for the chokra. I had to pay for all these expenses out of my monthly pay cheque of £17 – which was £3 per month more than a subaltern in the British Army. There was one more expense for those of us joining the Indian Army and that was the Munshi, who we were required to employ to teach us Urdu. He would come to each of us, in turn, during the afternoon to give us an hour's lesson. We did not make good scholars – preferring to rest, especially in the hotter stations. We paid him the regulation monthly fee of 30 rupees (£4 approx.). So, if you are quick on your mental arithmetic, you will have worked out that this left about £6 per month for everything else i.e. Mess Bill (e.g. all food) Club Bill, all drinks and sundries and we also paid something towards the regimental band.

Apart from our chummery, there was the officers' mess which was situated some 300 metres away and where we went to drink, relax, read papers, magazines and eat our meals. There were also the mess servants who had to be paid for by the officers. Apart from these expenses every military station or cantonment had a Club for sport and social purposes. Subscriptions and all drinks appeared on one's Club Bill at the end of each month and this in turn appeared on the mess bill which had to be paid by the 10th of the month – failure to do so meant a visit to the CO's office. Every British officer also civil servants (District Officers) and police would be expected to join this club, sometimes called a gymkhana.

Life in the Inniskillings was pretty happy-go-lucky, particularly for the officers who turned up at their offices more or less when they liked. Then at about 11a.m. we would slope off to the troops' canteen where a small cubby hole had been constructed of curtains and we would sit behind this, so as not to be seen by the troops, and drink until it was time to go to the officers' mess for lunch. Although War had been declared some weeks ago it really did not affect us at all. There was one officer who periodically had one of his 'weekends'. He would drink all day and night, come to the mess for meals, have each course served and then pushed it aside while he continued to drink vast quantities of gin. He would then be helped to his room by his bearer and would not be seen again until the next mealtime – when the procedure would be repeated.

A highland regiment stationed in Singapore, because of the perilous situation developing on account of the Japanese invasion there, had been ordered to send their families out of the area and it was decided that they should all be sent to join the Inniskillings' families in Wellington as there was sufficient spare family quarters in that cantonment. So now we had all the Scottish and Irish wives and families in one melting pot – and what a 'melting pot' it was, with plenty of trouble between the wives. Rightly or wrongly, our company commander, an out and out Irishman, had the warring wives brought into his office (accompanied by their respective but bashful husbands) and he really laid in to them in their own language!

When World War II broke out, (3 September 1939), a few days after we arrived in Wellington, I and another officer (Basil Seton) got a big surprise temporary posting. We were sent off to Madras and told to take over the censorship of all telegrams being sent by anyone – no codes of any description were allowed. We were allocated an office on the top floor of the General Post Office and told to get on with it! We two (both of us under 21 years of age) worked in 8 hour shifts, round the clock. We became most unpopular with the big businesses e.g. Banks, whose telegrams were all in code. The doors of the GPO were always left open so, as the night drew on, all the homeless people came in with their mats and spent the night on the floors and even on some of the desktops – all were well behaved but it was quite an adventure treading over all these bodies to get to and from our office each night!

One night we were invited to dinner at the Madras Club by one of the members. This club is one of the oldest in India. We turned up in dinner jackets but on arrival, the Head Waiter told us that we were improperly dressed and so our host, and we had to sit outside the dining room on the verandah. The proper dress for the Club was black jacket but with white trousers, and bow tie of course. In Calcutta it is the reverse, and Bombay it is white jacket and trousers. Fortunately our censorship job only lasted a couple of weeks after which we were relieved by two civilians, so we returned to Wellington.

Three of us pooled our resources and bought a Chrysler saloon car from one of the Inniskillings officers; we paid a total of £15 for it and, as it turned out, we were robbed. It used more water than petrol so we abandoned it after a month. I then bought a good large sporty Buick Straight '8' two-seater which lasted fairly well. I may well mention this car again at a later date. I took the driving test and passed – the Indian examiners would not have dared to fail any of us British Officers! The local Collector (Magistrate) had been at St Edward's School – but well before my time. This proved useful for a while but even with this connection he opted out of dealing with my various driving misdemeanours. On New Year's morning of the 1940 I managed to tear down one side of a bridge – there were three of us in the car and we were very lucky indeed as the left front wheel was overhanging the bridge from where there was a drop of about 8 metres down to the rocky riverbed. The magistrate refused to deal with my case but referred me to the Circuit judge who, fortunately, was a friend of my father in Cuttack, Orissa – where my father was the Inspector General of Police, so the matter was dropped, though I think I had to pay something towards the cost of repairs.

On Christmas morning there was a knock on my door and a man handed me a basket in which I found a bottle of whisky and 100 cigarettes. I went along to the others to inform them of my good luck and discovered that they too had received a basket of goodies. About half an hour later the Regimental Sergeant Major arrived and told us that the CO had ordered the surrender of these gifts which were to be returned to the donor who was, of course, the regimental contractor. Such presents were considered as a form of corruption and might influence our relations with the contractor in the future! On the subject of contractors let me explain, since I will be referring to them now and again. Away from the UK, units, be they army, navy or airforce, always employed, or rather signed on, a native contractor whose obligations would include many things but principally, the supply of foodstuffs, liquors for the canteen and officer's mess, laundry, repairs (boot and shoe), rental of furniture etc. They were always considered to be fairly well off but they liked to give the impression that they were grossly underpaid for their work and provisions. They also wanted to keep in the 'good books' of anyone who was not only in authority, but who might be in authority at some future date. This was very well realized and known throughout all the services, military or civilian and one had to be very careful not to receive gifts.

With the Inniskillings Fusiliers, we ULIA officers comprised 5 from the RMC, Sandhurst and two Indians from Dehru Dun (the Indian equivalent of Sandhurst) and very excellent men they were too. Although we British officers were more or less obliged to join the Club, the Indian officers were not allowed to – nor could any Anglo-Indians or British Other Ranks (BORs). They did not have much social life at all. In British regiments there were canteens and in the larger cantonments there might be a NAAFI (Naval, Army and Airforce Institute).

Of us seven ULIA, we fared as follows in the years ahead. Both the Indian officers were killed right at the beginning of the war during the Japanese invasion of Malaya. Of the remainder, one was killed in the MEF on the fall back to Alamein, one had his jaw shot away in Burma when his position was overrun by the Japanese and he was left for dead – however he struggled back to our lines, had a replacement jaw fitted and then, later, won the Middle Weight Boxing championship of the Western Command. He had been captain of the Boxing team I was in whilst at Sandhurst. Another got three bullets in his stomach while on a patrol near Enfidaville, Tunisia, but managed to crawl back to his unit and was then invalided out. Another one, even as a 20 year old, was very irascible and, according to reports, did not improve as the years went by. He was pushed from unit to unit after which I don't know what happened to him. That only leaves me – who, apart from one or two headaches occasioned by enemy fire and maybe the odd tot of whisky – well – I survived completely unscathed! Perhaps I was lucky or just careful?

Chapter 3 : 1940

India, Joining the Indian Army, Holiday to Kashmir

On account of the state of war (1939/45), our attachment (as ULIA) was cut short and the postings to our Indian regiments came through. I was posted to the 16th Punjab Regiment – their 3rd bn. (battalion). Each regiment had 5 bns. so now I was in the 3/16 Punjab Regiment. In early January 1940, having left the Inniskillings in Wellington, I had a very long rail journey to join my Indian Regiment which was stationed in Karachi, (Sind). This journey involved going down to Madras, then up the East coast of India to Calcutta, then north-west all the way to Delhi, up to Lahore and finally south down to Karachi. As the journey could take over 7 days I decided to stop on the way and stay with my parents for a few days in Cuttack, (Orissa) where my father held the post as Inspector General of Police. I eventually arrived at Karachi station to be met by the adjutant. He had a car in which to take me to my quarters. My luggage was loaded on to a wheeled platform pulled by one of the regimental camels and came along later. My room here was in the usual chummery – six rooms on two floors – I was allotted a ground floor room that was much the same as the one that I had vacated in Wellington with the same furniture. One soon settled down! I had to take on a different bearer and chokra as my previous ones would not come to this part of the India.

Life at Karachi was an eye-opener in many ways. Soon after arrival I was informed that all newly joined officers must go round all the married quarters and drop a visiting card through the letterboxes. I had had some cards printed before leaving England on the advice of my parents. These cards had to be delivered personally in the early afternoon in the heat of the day – on a bicycle (junior officers did not possess cars), while the recipients were having an afternoon nap. This was soon followed by an invitation to dinner – wearing dinner jackets was obligatory of course. One was told who to drop these cards off at, including officers (and their wives) of other regiments and also, perhaps some senior civilians of various sorts. Karachi, being the capital of the Sind province had a Governor, so we had to leave one at Government House. Whenever you went 'out of station' you had to leave another card and one again when you returned – that way the ADCs would know who was present and therefore who had to be given invitations for Government House functions – at which, during the daytime at garden parties etc. white gloves must be worn regardless of the heat and a hat carried in one hand.

I failed to leave a card for one of our middle-aged officers because I went away on leave and then was sent to the Middle East. When I returned after four years of warfare in the MEF, the wife cut me dead and would not speak to me!

The first day I reported to the CO's office he greeted me warmly and then, in the same breath, asked what bank overdraft I had accrued in my short time in India, so I told him. He then went on to outline how I would reduce and finish this overdraft and I was to report to him monthly how the plan was progressing. Sure enough I was in the clear three months later! I was also told that I would be attached to a Mussulman (Muslim) company commanded by a major so I went off and introduced myself to him. He was about forty years of age and seemed quite a nice chap. He told me that the first parade was at 6.30a.m. The following morning, bearing in mind what I had gleaned about the time officers turned up for parades in the Inniskillings, I thought I would be very zealous and turn up but only 10 minutes or so late. Lo and behold when I got there he was pacing up and down and pointed out to me that officers should always be on time, so the next morning I thought I would be even more zealous and beat him to it and turned up dead on 6.30a.m. But then he reprimanded me for not being 5 minutes early as all officers should be. This was a lesson I have never forgotten and even now always aim to be early for all appointments – much to my wife's fury!

In these memoirs, when I refer to India or Indians I mean pre-partition India. The sub-continent then consisted of present day India, Pakistan,

Bangladesh, Kashmir and also Ceylon. As far as we were concerned the inhabitants were all Indians in those days. The Indian Army must not be confused with the Army in India. The latter included everyone – British and Indian troops. The Indian Army regiments consisted of 20 Infantry regiments (each with 5 bns.), the 10 Gurkhas regiments (each with 2 bns.), about 20 Cavalry Regiments and 4 regiments of Sappers and Miners. The Indian regiments each had various castes. The 16th Punjab Regiment for example had 50% Mussulmans, 25% Sikhs (Hindus) and 25% Dogras (Hindus); this was in keeping with the British policy of "divide & rule". All the officers were British and there were only 12 of them. In addition there were VCOs (Viceroys Commissioned Officers) who were Indians who had come up through the ranks. There were three ranks of VCOs – the Subedar Major (equivalent to the British rank of RSM), then came the Subedar (with two pips on his shoulder) and was 2i/c of a Company and finally a Jemadar with one pip – a platoon commander. They were all junior to any British Commissioned officer – regardless of length of service. To become a VCO a man would have served at least 20 years, probably more – and very fine soldiers they were too.

The Indian regiments were almost entirely recruited from what were called the 'martial races'. They were all agricultural workers, land owners etc., none at all from the cities. They would come very largely from the Punjab (Land of Five Rivers), Rajputana Gujerat and the Maharratas. The cities provided the Sappers and Miners, as they were more literate. The Indian (and Ghurkha) soldiers, except a few who became clerks, were on the whole illiterate even in their own tongue. Except in the case of the Ghurkha regiments, where they spoke Ghurkhali, the *lingua franca* of the Indian regiments was Urdu.

All officers were required to learn this and in some regiments they were also expected to learn the dialects of the region from which their men were recruited, e.g. Pushtu and Gurmuki. In those days, before I joined the Indian Army, a newly joined officer was expected to spend his first year two-month leave entitlement visiting the recruiting catchments areas for their regiment. He would set off with his civilian bearer and military orderly, on horseback, and visit the many villages from where his regiment recruited men. He would stay in the villages and get to know what their life was like and improve his knowledge of their language and customs.

The strength of only 12 British Officers meant they were hardly ever all present at one time – as one might be on two-month annual leave, another on six months leave to the UK, one would almost always be attending a course somewhere and another would be detached for Staff Duties etc. Since each company (five to a bn.) had a Major or Captain in command, any junior officer, notwithstanding his junior rank, would be required to take over from absent senior officers. The rank and pay unfortunately did not go with this temporary upgrading! In my case, my company commander went off on leave almost immediately and so I became a company commander – with only 2 weeks' service behind me. Before long the other company commanders also went off and before I knew what was happening I became the commander of four companies (400 men approx) – at the tender age of 20. It never occurred to me that I couldn't do the job. I had, of course, the Subedars of these companies to advise me, and also an English speaking clerk. I now knew the purpose of the one-year ULIA learning attachment to British regiments!

In the evening we would go and play hockey with the men and this was on hard pitches similar to hard tennis courts. Joining the station gymkhana club was obligatory for officers in India. These clubs provided the social life and certain sport facilities e.g. golf, tennis, swimming etc. They were reserved entirely for English members – no Indians at all – even if they were officers in the Indian units in the same station.

We would go to the officers' mess every evening for dinner. The dress was formal with dinner jackets five days a week and full mess uniform on one night. On Sunday we could go in a suit. No coats were allowed off even on the hottest of nights – and there were plenty of those. The bearer of each officer would have to be present in his best dress and turban and he would stand behind his officer and serve him only. There would also be two or three mess servants. So if there were only four to dinner on a night there would be at least six bearers on duty. On formal mess nights there would be about six to eight pipers playing their bagpipes while marching around behind our chairs – what a noise! These mess nights were always followed with some rather, what even I considered, childish games: "Are you there McGarity?"; "Do you know that muffin man, do you know his name?" etc.

In July 1940 I was due for 2 months' leave – I had been with the regiment for only just over five months. Because by now the shipping arrangements back to the UK were much restricted by the war, my parents could not return there so they decided to holiday up in Kashmir instead. My two sisters were up there with them so I decided to join them all, especially as my father undertook to pay for my hotel accommodation.

It was a very pleasant and happy holiday and I celebrated my 21st birthday up in Gulmurg which was very crowded for, like my parents, there were many people who were due to go back to the UK but were not able to because of the war. The distant war, of course, hung over everybody as did the atmosphere. Before my two months were up I was recalled to the bn. and so I returned to Karachi.

Chapter 4 : 1940

Secunderabad (Deccan)

The whole bn. moved down to Secunderabad – a long four or five-day journey. Secunderabad was another military cantonment in the state of what was then called Hyderabad. The Head of the State was the Nizam who was reputedly the richest man in the world at that time. His Prime Minister was one called Nawab Salah Jung, also very wealthy. He invited me to a dinner one night. It was during the Ramadan period so none of the guests, mostly Muslims, had touched food all day. When night arrived we all fell to with great gusto. There were about twenty men present but no women, of course, as they were in purdah. I do recall seeing a well-known sculpted figurine of a standing women with a veil across her face all in marble but one could see her face through the veil, also of marble.

While in Secunderabad the regiment used to carry out route marches through the countryside, particularly the villages – with the band playing. This was what was known as 'showing the flag', in other words making the army's presence felt to the people – as a warning? We used to carry out this chore when I was with the Inniskillings.

In Secunderabad our CO left us for promotion and we got another one who arrived all keen to make his presence felt, and we were made to do afternoon parades – unheard in pre-war India! He also made us newly joined subalterns buy the very expensive mess dress even though there was a war on. I wore it once. The first full dress mess night after I got this uniform I put it on with great pride and set off for the officer's mess – on my bicycle. The mess was about a quarter of a mile away but on the way I had to pass the VCO's mess .My passage was stopped by my Sikh Jemadar who waved to me join him for a drink. This was to be my downfall. I had quite a few drinks, each one being the equivalent of triple measure in an English pub – he then plied me with curry and rice and then sent me on my way. By the time I arrived at the mess, riding very groggily on my bike, I was late and the 2i/c said so in no uncertain terms – we never liked each other at the best of times. We then all went into dinner. It was a very hot night so all the windows were open. What with the heat, the mess uniform AND all the whisky and curry and rice, I did not last long and had to rush out into the night to be violently sick – but more unfortunately I chose to do so near one of the open windows and so the other officers were unlucky enough, if not to witness, then to hear everything. The next day I was regaled by my friends who gave a detailed description of the night's proceedings and my part in them! Before leaving this subject I would tell you that I never wore that suit again as I was sent off to the Middle East, but before leaving I sent off all my unwanted baggage to be stored in the Regimental depot at Sialkot. Four years or so later when I returned to India and went to collect my things, I found that this expensive mess dress had been entirely eaten away – only the brass buttons were left.

Chapter 5 : 1940

Going to War in the MEF (Middle East Forces)

When my bn. (the 3/16th Punjab) was stationed in Secunderabad (Deccan) I was sent off on a 6 week Small Arms course to Saugar but after two weeks was recalled back and on arrival was told that I had been posted to the 4th bn. as a reinforcement. This bn. was already in the Middle East as part of the 7th Indian Brigade that in turn was in the 4th Indian Division. I was disappointed to hear this but not surprised as I had fallen foul of the 2 i/c and, with the arrival of a new CO, no doubt he gave his opinion as to who should be selected and sent to the MEF. In the event this turned out to be a very lucky move for me for, shortly after I left, the 3rd bn. was sent off to Malaya where it was overrun by the Japs and the whole bn. became POWs (prisoners of war) – many of whom never survived the rigours of the Jap camps and working parties. Before I left the bn., I had to take steps to arrange the transport of my Buick car, which I had left behind in Wellington on my departure to join my Indian regiment, in Karachi. This involved paying a driver to go all the way to Wellington to pick up the car, and keep it filled with petrol. I don't remember how much this all cost, but I do remember that I did not have enough money. So I went and did quite the wrong thing and asked the contractor to lend me the amount involved – he, of course, was very willing to do this. A day or so later, when the driver had gone off I related what I had done to a couple of other officers, not much more senior than myself. They were horrified and told me in no uncertain terms what a heinous thing I had done and told me to go back and return the money to the contractor immediately and they made arrangements to lend me the money themselves. On the arrival back of my car I repaid my debt to them and then left for the MEF.

On or about December 1, I was due to leave by boat from Bombay and on arrival there was put in charge of about sixty Sepoys also going out there as reinforcements for the bn. The journey was uneventful and we came alongside the dock at Suez on the 9th December 1940 – the very day that Wavell started his successful push along the North coast of Africa. The Italians had previously advanced eastwards along the coast towards Egypt and occupied Sidi Barrani. However Wavell's push, using only two brigades of the 4th Ind. Div., swept round behind the Italians and captured many thousands then beat them back across the frontier past Sollum.

Thereafter the Australians took on the chase and the 4th Ind. Div. was free to be used elsewhere. I was not involved in this campaign at all. Having disembarked at Suez, we reinforcements were taken to the Indian reinforcement camp at Mena – about one mile from the Pyramids, which could be easily seen and there we waited to be called up.

On this sea journey, as I said, I was taking a number of Sepoy reinforcements which included Sikhs, who for religious reasons, did not, and would not smoke or touch tobacco. I had picked a very large Sikh as my orderly – a great chap he was too. One day I was sitting on deck and, absentmindedly asked him to go and get my cigarettes from my cabin. He was a very long time doing this but eventually turned up holding a sandbag that he had filled with sand from a fire bucket, in the bottom of which was my tin of cigarettes! As the years and the war rolled on, they (the Sikhs) became less and less orthodox until in the end, when I was commanding a Sikh company, they all knew that I was a very heavy smoker and each section would carry a packet of cigarettes to offer me while I doing the rounds! Another quite interesting fact was that the Hindus and Muslim Sepoys would not drink water from the same tap as each other, so the water trucks had to have two taps fitted, one on each side (from the same water supply!) and then everyone was happy. This practice was also to die a natural death as the war wore on. A good Muslim would follow the dictates of Islam and pray five times a day – though this is not compulsory in war. In spite of this many did – but they became fewer and fewer.

This Mena Camp (the Indian MEF Reinforcement Camp) was set out near the Pyramids and below them was the Mena House Hotel, which became famous as the site for one of Churchill's summit meetings with Roosevelt and Chiang Kai-shek, during World War II.

I happened to go to the hotel on Christmas Day (1940) with a view to joining in whatever celebrations that might be available. There was much celebrating going on in the 'well' of the hotel which had an overlooking verandah and balustrade running round it. I chanced to look up and saw two little girls peering down wistfully; I went off to the bar and got two glasses of soft drinks that I took up, and joined them for 15 or 20 minutes. One was about 14 years of age and the other younger – I then returned to my friends down below.

The years passed and I went off to the Eritrean and Western Desert Campaigns. Three, or maybe four years later, when I must have changed very considerably since this episode, I was on a short, three-day leave to the fleshpots in Alexandria and while there attended the wedding of a friend who was marrying one of the many cosmopolitan girls who happened to reside in those towns. At the reception I felt a tap on my shoulder and looked round to see a very pretty and mature young girl. She asked me if I recognized her and when I ruefully confessed that I did not, she then reminded me of that Christmas Day in 1940 at the Mena House Hotel. She said that she had never forgotten my going up to join her and her sister and recognized me as soon as she set her eyes on me. What a memory!

Historically Egypt, somewhat unwillingly, was on our side. Prior to the war the Italians had tried to build an empire and had not only taken possession of Libya but also Eritrea/Ethiopia in the horn of Africa. In North Africa they had constructed a barbed wire fence, about one and a half metres high and 2 metres wide, as a frontier demarcation line between Libya and Egypt. It ran due South down from the coast at a point called Halfaya Pass or Solum and it went on down until it reached the Sahara desert. There were one or two gaps along its length – one in particular was situated about fifteen miles from the coast. This was near an old Roman well called Bir Shefferzen. These wells were shaped like a flask i.e. narrow at the top and which then spread out to quite a large cavern below. On top, alongside the entrance, a large mound, 'bir', would be heaped up so that it could easily be recognized from a distance. I shall return to this 'gap' later on in the next desert campaign. Now, I would point out that, westwards from the Nile delta right up to the border with Libya was what was called the Western Desert and our forces in that area went under the name of the Wes Des Force. It was not until much later on, two or three years, that Montgomery arrived and changed the name to the 8th Army.

Before continuing I thought that I would say something about the social life in the Middle East, North Africa, Cyprus and Italy during the war years. Much the same class distinction as prevailed in India was carried over. All the best hotels, bars and cabarets were reserved for officers only. The other ranks had to find other places of interest. This ruling was not official – just an accepted practice and I don't recall any trouble caused by it, though the New Zealanders and Australians were a bit irked since their ranks included many ex-members of the professions e.g. bankers, accountants, farmers, solicitors, shop owners etc. This distinction even included brothels where MPs (Military Police) were put on duty outside officers' brothels to ensure that ORs did not try to enter.

Chapter 6 : 1941

Eritrean Campaign

Wavell, as C-in-C of the Middle East, decided that he could not leave the Italians unmolested in the Horn of Africa where they posed a constant threat to his supply lines and also perhaps the oil supplies from the Persian (Iranian) oil fields. He planned an invasion eastwards from the Sudan towards the very unfriendly terrain of Eritrea and Ethiopia with Cheren as the main focus of the attack. The 4th Indian Div. was allocated this task against a vastly superior (in numbers) force of Italians and Eritreans. Two brigades were detailed off to carry out this audacious plan. The third brigade (7th Ind. Brig.) was given the task of advancing south down from the Sudanese port of Port Suakin and attacking the Italians from that direction and thereby threatening them on a further front. In so doing so they would have to withdraw some of their forces in front of the other two brigades. It was described on the BBC news as the "romantic littoral column!"

The 7th Brigade (including the 4/16 Punjabis & the Royal Sussex) was taken out of the Western Desert and sent down to the Sudan. This Brigade also included a French colonial bn. from Chad, a detachment from the French Foreign Legion and another from the Sudan Defence Force. It was then that I was sent to join the bn., which I did. At that moment the bn. was camped out near Omdurman between the Nile and the White Nile. It was not long after I joined that the Brigade set off on its allotted task.

How they went I don't recall, but I know what happened to me. I was put in command of 'B' Company of Muslim Sepoys. I was just over 21 years of age but I was blessed with an old soldier as my second-in-command (2i/c) namely one Subedar Daim Khan – a man with very long service (about 27 years). I travelled down in transport having been told that my company would be sailing down the Red Sea (in native dhows) from Port Suakin to a place reputed to be another port by the name of Mersa Taklai. This turned out to be just a broken down concrete jetty which had seen better days, and that was it, no buildings whatsoever.

Eventually my very seasick Sepoys arrived. In the meanwhile the Royal Sussex had been engaged with the enemy – and taken many prisoners, including two Italian officers. They had also sustained some casualties. I had started my war experiences! One of the wounded was a Captain Jack de Manio – who was later awarded a MC (Military Cross). He was quite a character and one to whom I will return later.

After a while I was sent transport to carry my men and me south and we joined the rest of the bn. in a dry riverbed. The terrain was very hilly, with deep, dry sandy ravines and very little water. Once on the move we had to press on without our motor transport and make do with what seemed like hundreds of camels – this was because we were confined in space to the dry 'nullahs'. These camels made an awful noise with their grunting and groaning and passed on their ticks to us as we were all sleeping on the ground. There was a lot of game about, leopards, guinea fowls etc. One morning my orderly pointed out some leopard's pugmarks, which showed that during the night, a family of them had passed by within a few feet of my sleeping spot.

The enemy was retreating slowly from the hills towards Cheren. One day we had to do a long march along one of these hot dry 'nullahs' and my men, becoming very thirsty, had drunk much water. We were only issued with one water bottle per man per day for all purposes. When we finally got to where the rest of the bn. was encamped I asked the CO if we could have some more water. He refused initially; however he relented and we were all given a top-up for our bottles.

I had marched ahead of the company with my Subedar (Daim Khan) at the back to keep the men moving. He was a wonderful man and, although he was junior to me he would never show any disrespect whatsoever and I looked up to him no end asking his advice on many matters. Although he could not speak English he seemed to understand what was being said.

Anyway, as I said, he was at the back so did not arrive where we were halted until we had received the extra water. When the CO told him what I/we had done, Daim Khan made the men and myself stand up, called us to attention and ordered us all to take the stoppers out of our water bottles. Then he made us tip the bottles upside down and let the precious water pour out on to the sand. Not a word was said. I learned a salutary lesson from him regarding water discipline and much more from him thereafter.

He was much admired by the men as well, (A couple of years later, when we were in Cyprus and he was a prisoner of war from Benghazi, I reckoned my men were taking too long to perform a certain task so I said to them that they wouldn't be so slow if Subedar Daim Khan had been there and that proved enough to get them moving in double quick time – even though he was safely in a POW camp thousands of miles away!).

One day I was given orders to capture a high hill, named Enghiat. There was another company involved – they were Dogras, hillmen from the lower slopes of the Himalayas and very agile up and down hills. Their company commander had been serving in one of the princely states forces and therefore not as fit as the rest of his men. When we got to the top of the hill we found that the enemy had fled but when I went to talk to this other officer, his subedar told me that the 'sahib' had not made the ascent. It appeared that the climb/attack had affected him mentally and he was sent back to India and eventually to a mental asylum from which he never recovered. The next day our Quartermaster (Tiny Marr) decided he would come and visit me on the top of this mountain. He was an 'old man' of at least thirty-five years of age, overweight as well and had been a tea planter before volunteering for war service. I watched him as he arrived at my position. When he got close to me and while we were talking, suddenly a blood vessel exploded from his forehead and the blood shot all over me! He was a very game chap. Later, in the desert, he drove over a mine which exploded and smashed both his legs and that was the last I saw of him.

A few days later, while on this mountaintop, I was ordered to put in an attack on the enemy who had repositioned themselves further along the crest. My company was to be accompanied by another, whose commander was a Bertie Herbert (an officer with the most perfect command of the English language I have ever heard). He was killed later at the battle of Sidi Omar. The crest of this mountain was often in the clouds in the early morning and the aspect was as if one was looking down from an aircraft. Just before the attack Bertie and I were standing looking into the clouds in front of us when they lifted very suddenly and we were caught there right out in the open. As soon as the enemy saw us they started firing in our direction, so we rapidly took cover. The attack was due to take place soon afterwards. My Subedar Daim Khan asked me where I would be during the attack. I said I would be with the reserve platoon at the back. At Sandhurst we had been taught that company commanders should come up behind with the reserve platoon so that they might be able to influence the result of an operation by utilising the reserve. He gave me a stare and said, "No, Sahib – you must go in front and be an example to the men". I took his advice and thereafter always stayed well in front of my men during the rest of my service – but I would mention here that this was the normal practice in the Indian Army. At the appointed time both of our companies advanced with bayonets fixed. This proved too much for the opposition who retreated as fast as they could. We sustained only one casualty.

The enemy then disappeared altogether from this area and retreated towards Cheren I presume. I am a bit vague now as to what happened next. Anyhow the brigade went over to the left side (east) and arrived by the shores of the Red Sea and then advanced onto the port of Massawa where there was another attack, in which my company was not involved. We had one officer casualty – he was shot through the chest, but in due course lived to be evacuated back to India. The port was captured at about the same time as Cheren fell. And that was the end of the Eritrean campaign. The brigade was then shipped back to Egypt and the Western Desert.

Chapter 7 : 1941

Western Desert Campaign (Crusader), Omars, Onto Benghazi

After the Eritrean campaign all the 4th Ind. Div. was taken out and returned to the Western Desert where the various units were allocated defensive areas in case the Italians decided to invade Egypt again. We, in the 7th Ind. Infantry brigade, were allotted to a small bay about seventy miles west from Alexandria. It was called Bagush. We took up positions in a semicircle around it with the sea making up the northern flank. There was a railway line from the (Nile) delta and one road. We, the 4/16 PR, were allocated a segment of this perimeter and had to dig slit trenches as part of this defensive zone. The Western Desert itself was a long plateau about twenty metres above sea level with a rocky cliff dropping down to the sea.

The Desert Train. Throughout the Western Desert campaigns there was only the one railway line which ran from Cairo, through Alexandria and then on along the North African coast to Mersa Matruh, Alamein and thence to Sidi Barrani. The main road also ran alongside this line so it was a prime target for the enemy aircraft. Apart from supplies being brought up to the forward areas this line also provided a means for men to be sent back to the Delta (Alexandria/Cairo) on short (very short) leaves.

It was not allowed any lights so, once on board, one could do nothing except sit and wait until we reached our destination. I cannot remember how long the journey took – about 20 hours I should think.

The authorities never could work out what was the best time the train should leave Cairo. For, whatever time was tried, it never seemed to be the right one. Everyone returning to the Desert wanted to have quite a few drinks before setting off, as there was no facilities on the train. So – nearly everyone was either inebriated or near to being so. All this activity in the pitch dark did not lend itself to 'good order and military discipline'. Other articles have been written about this Desert Train as it came to be known. The corridor was always crammed full of baggage and to get to the loo one had to clamber along the top of this luggage.

I digress here. As a schoolboy, as I have outlined already, I was brought up by guardians who also took in other boys. One of a pair of brothers was Arthur Paton. On leaving school he went on up to Oxford University and when war broke out he joined the 11th Hussars (called the Cherry pickers on account of the pink/maroon coloured trousers they wore on full dress parades). On one of my return trips back from Cairo, I was crawling along on top of all the baggage and came face to face with Arthur who was emerging from the loo. Again, about a year later, I was in Cairo and decided to visit the Turf Club. Later that evening I went down to the loo and once again found myself standing next to Arthur. Yet again, later on in the desert, when I was wandering around with my intelligence section I saw an armoured car far away, but at that distance I could not tell whether it was one of 'ours'. When I saw an individual go apart from the vehicle I rushed forward and discovered it was Arthur relieving himself – so I joined him! Many years later, after the war was over I had departed from India and was going out to the Rhodesias. The ship stopped at the port of Nairobi. As we had a few hours to while away the time we went ashore and then onto a seaside hotel. When we got there I decided that I wanted to go to the loo – which was sited downstairs. On positioning myself I found I was standing next to – whom? Arthur Paton, of course!

Going back to our defensive position on the escarpment. There were a few caves that had been used by Bedouins. I thought I would settle down in one of these, as it would provide some cover from the sand storms etc. This turned out to be a bad mistake for I soon discovered that it was infested by fleas –very large and voracious ones.

In the morning I built a fire in the cave, closed the entrance and let the fire burn for a few hours hoping the smoke would kill off the fleas. I was wrong, for when I returned to the cave for the night I was bitten all over the place. So I gave up and returned to the normal slit trench, which was rather more than a metre in depth over which a groundsheet was erected and sand thrown over the sides. This kept the perpetual sand drifts from invading one's sleeping hours. The Officer's mess tent was always constructed by having a trench dug in a 'U' shape, the trench being rather less than a metre deep, the tent was erected over this in the normal way, with the sides covered over with sand. The centre of the 'U' was used as the table and we would sit round it with our feet in the trench. If we were going to be bombed from the air then all we had to do was sink down into the trench. Sand storms, bad or mediocre storms were a common occurrence and so we got used to them. In this defensive position – which we called a 'box' – the Bagush box – life was very quiet as the front line was about 50 miles away with no one doing very much. I asked the CO if I could take charge of the Signal Platoon and learn signalling. In those days we relied on five forms of communication:

'Flag wagging' – semaphore with flags.

Heliograph – a contraption with a mirror on a tripod which one would aim at a distant station also with a helio, and the reflected sun would provide the light with which we would then send messages by a form of morse code (long and short flashes). This means of communication could travel great distances – up to 80 miles it was said; of course there had to be sunlight – and it was not much use in Europe.

Torch light – a lamp erected on a tripod, messages would be sent by similar Morse code of long and short flashes.

Telephone. Either by speech or, very often, by code using the normal Morse code of dots and dashes.

And finally by:

Wireless (No. 18 set) –these were comparatively new to us in 1941 and were used for speech and, sometimes Morse code.

Typical Western Desert scene. Flat, featureless, hard rocky surface.

From my slit trench I graduated to a more spacious dugout, which I shared with another officer. It was wide enough for two camp beds with a space in-between us and over the top we erected a sheet of corrugated iron. It was deep enough to stand up in. One day the worst sand storm I ever experienced blew up. We could see it coming – a great black wall which, when it hit us, enveloped us in darkness and, of course, blinding sand. There was nothing for it but to sit it out and this we did for some hours. Unbeknown to us the sand was building up on top of our dugout so much so, that the weight of the sand on top eventually proved too much for the cross beam and corrugated roof which collapsed. Fortunately I was standing up at the time but the roof scraped down my back – however I was all right, but the other chap was completely pinned down with sand and I had to get help to dig him out.

There was not much time and even less opportunity to go romancing during the war in the Middle East. I had one go at it. I was sent back to Cairo with a bout of bronchitis, flu etc. I was admitted to the Scottish General Military Hospital on Gezira Island and there I was lucky to have a very nice nurse (called Betty) to look after me. Eventually I was discharged and returned to my unit in the desert. Six months or so later I was granted the usual three days short leave so I wrote to Betty and asked her if she would come out with me – I would telephone her when I arrived in Cairo. Before telephoning her I made arrangements to have a table booked at the famous Shepherds Hotel, where I was staying. This hotel was a very popular meeting place. She said she would meet me in the foyer of the hotel at a given time. She duly arrived, but when I said that I had booked a table at this well-attended venue, she did not seem to be very keen and suggested that we got to a less well-known restaurant – off the beaten track. So we got to another place but I got the feeling that she was on tenterhooks throughout the meal. I got around to thinking that perhaps she had a boyfriend of a more permanent nature and probably stationed in Cairo and whom she did not want to meet whilst with me. Anyway, the meal over, I called up a taxi, and took her back to her lodgings, which happened to be on a houseboat (on the Nile) for nurses, we shook hands and I departed. Nurses were warned to be careful of officers who had been a long time in the desert – with no female company! In passing I would mention that some time later Churchill came out to the Middle East where he was taken very ill and a nurse was allocated to look after him – the nurse was this Betty!

While in the box the brigade was required to dig trenches to form a 'D' shape around the coastline. Digging in this part of the desert was not easy on account of the hard rocky substrata. A keen RE (Royal Engineer) officer thought to speed things up a bit and started a competition to see who could dig the most trenches in a set time. One day there was a howling desert storm and Bertie Herbert and I were standing up supervising our rather reluctant men when this officer turned up and asked if he could measure the depth of our trenches. This was too much for Bertie, who with his great eloquence turned on this unfortunate man and said, "My good fellow, if you think that this is a good time to indulge in your craving for mathematical exactitude while the atmosphere is permeated with particles of silica – I don't!" whereupon he strode off into the blinding sand storm leaving a much chastened RE officer gawping after him.

I will mention here that while we were in this part of the Western Desert the 5th Ind. Brigade, from our Division, were doing great things in Syria where they fought and defeated the Vichy French forces.

Apart from the signal platoon activities I also asked the CO if I could take over the Intelligence Section consisting of eight or nine men. Their duties were not clearly defined but mostly concerned with the updating of the situation maps in the CO's office/dugout. This turned out to be a very good move on my part as I began to take a great interest in map reading – particularly of the nearby and more distant areas of the desert. I would be left alone to do what I wanted – no interference from anyone. So I used to get my section into a truck and off we would go for days at a time. Planning routes here, there and everywhere, practising using the oil and sun compasses and travelling by night as well; in the end we all became very proficient – a proficiency that would stand me (and others) in very good stead later. To the south of the box some forty miles away the Sahara proper started; it was also called the 'sea of sand' for the dunes rose up high above the coastal region. It was thought that perhaps the enemy might be entering into this area, coming round our left flank and getting into the delta area behind us. In fact they never did do this, though our LRDG (Long Range Desert Group) did it with devastating effect on the enemies' lines of communication and airfields. The sea of sand was well named as the sand rolled way into the distance like huge waves. It had high ridges with sheer drops on one or the other side. The sand was very soft and in a vehicle, one could not use brakes for if you did, the wheels would just sink in making it very difficult to get started again. We soon found a way of preventing this happening, and if so, how to get out of the trouble. There had been an (RE) detachment whose job it was to patrol into the Sahara but they made the mistake of driving too hard and fast up to one of the high dunes and not realizing that there was a sheer drop on the far side, their truck flew though air and came crashing down. The officer in charge was very badly hurt with both legs broken, and was evacuated to a hospital. I was then given the job. I would go out with my section and we would drive about fifty miles straight into the Sahara and just look around for any tracks that would surely have been made by anyone passing along. We never did see any but I enjoyed the absolute peace and quiet out there – day and night, and of course, there was the added relief from the ever present flies. I had two experiences out there. One day, we did see some black objects in the distance and I drove over to see what they could be. They turned out be fragments of petrified trees from some very distant past when this area has been afforested. On another occasion I had stopped at the top of one of the high ridges of sand. Looking down I noticed a small black object on the surface, about a metre down from where I was standing. I took a step down to pick it up and there was an enormous roaring noise, quite deafening. My first reaction was that some bombs had been dropped nearby, but this seemed unlikely. A few years later I was reading a book about travels in a desert (by a woman, perhaps Freya Stark) and she also had this same experience – rarely heard or at least recorded by anyone. She explained that the roaring noise was caused by the movement of great masses of sand activated by someone or something which had moved the sand, in my case, by stepping down to pick up the object, which, in the event, turned out be just the shell of a beetle.

Some of my patrolling had been in a westerly direction towards the Libyan (Italian) frontier and I got to know what few landmarks there were. I also patrolled at night, over the border wire into enemy territory – in my truck. Once, one misty early morning, we were returning from a foray when suddenly I saw a vehicle coming towards us. As it drew up alongside I saw that they were Germans. Not thinking, I gave them a wave and they waved back to us and then we were both gone!

Life continued to be fairly quiet but we all knew that the Western Desert C-in-C, General Auchinlech, was planning a 'push'. Sure enough this was to begin on November 22, 1941 under the code name CRUSADER, and the 4th Ind. Div. was going to be heavily involved – with the 7th Ind. Brigade leading.

The Italians – with some detachment of newly arrived Germans, had built a defensive line about the Solum area and particularly around two places know as the Omars (Omar Nuovo and Libyan Omar) where they dug themselves into a very strong box – as we had ourselves done elsewhere. As I recounted previously the Italians had before the war, constructed a deep barbed wire frontier wire fence running south from Solum. The brigade (which included the Royal Sussex, the 4/11th Sikhs and ourselves the 4/16th PR) was detailed off to capture the Omars and to do this we were going to advance to the south of the Omars, passing through the frontier fence gap at Bir Shefferzen and circling round to the back of the enemy's defensive position then attacking down from the north.

I was ordered to navigate the whole brigade all the way to the start point of the attack – in the pitch dark. The brigade started off in daylight in desert open formation, then as it grew dark, all the hundreds of vehicles slowly closed in towards each other until they could just keep each other in sight – no lights were allowed of course, except I had to have one torch shining backwards so that most vehicles could keep an eye on my direction. We proceeded along at about 5 mph. I had taken the precaution of taking three of my men out in the early evening and told them to go to the Bir Shefferzen gap as soon as it was dark, sit there and then, at a given time, to flash a torch in the direction from which we were coming. The responsibility was very great and I could not afford to make any mistake on such an important occasion. Anyhow everything went according to plan and we all arrived at this small gap. Having passed through the Brigade pressed on with me leading. I was a bit worried as to how close I was leading the column to the enemy box so I sent out a couple of my men to the right, to report if I was too close – but they never came back. We could not wait, so pressed on once again making the wide sweep to the north and then back eastwards to get to the attacking start line. Remember all this took place in the pitch dark and it was to be a silent attack – for which the 4th Div. became famous.

As the dawn came up the enemy became fully aware of what was about to happen and opened up with artillery and machine gun fire on the Royal Sussex as they pushed their way into the defences. Attached to the brigade was a squadron of ‘I’ Matilda tanks, which were then considered almost unstoppable, as their armour was thicker than any other tanks – but they were very slow indeed. The Royal Sussex, with the tanks in support, managed to take the first two or three lines of trenches after receiving very heavy casualties including most of the tanks. Then it was the turn of the 4/16th. We had to wheel right towards another defensive position. Having finished my work of navigation I reported back to the CO to await any orders he might want to give me. Unknown to us the Germans had brought up a new weapon – an 88mm gun which could be used as artillery, as an anti-aircraft gun and finally, but by no means least, as an anti-tank gun. This gun was to have a big influence throughout the war, especially when it was mounted on their Tiger tanks. In the Omars, I believe, they only had the one 88mm gun but it was responsible for knocking out all our ‘I’ tanks.

Our two leading companies were standing around waiting to go into the attack. One company commander (John McGarity) was champing at the bit to get cracking. I was standing with him and we could hear and almost feel the machine bullets whistling past and over us. Bullets at the start of their flight are going faster than the speed of sound and so give a loud crack as they go overhead but as they slow down their passing becomes a whisper. John just stood there with his scarf flying in the wind as if nothing in particular was happening. Eventually the CO gave him the go ahead and off he went with his company into a hail of bullets with the remaining two 'I' tanks.

I am a bit vague as to what happened then. I know that news came back that some of the trenches had been taken, that McGarity had been killed and that the advance had come to a halt. The CO, adjutant and I went forwards and got down into one of the captured trenches and that became the bn. HQ for the next few days. Either that day or the next, the CO told me that one of our mortar detachments had taken up a position behind one of the stopped 'I' tanks and was firing onto the enemy positions, but that it was running out of ammunition and I was to take some more up using a small thin skinned troop carrier. I loaded up and then headed towards the 'I' tank that I could see in the not so far distance. As I was drawing near and coming up behind the tank, I could hear shells going over my carrier and landing around me as I went forward. I decided that sitting in the carrier with all that ammunition next to me was not a good place to be, so I told the driver to stop and yelled to him to bale out – quick. As we both landed on the ground a shell from the German 88mm hit the carrier and exploded many of its contents – which continued to explode for some time onwards. I found the mortar section in fairly good heart considering the very nasty place they were in. They were not alone, for the surviving members of the 'I' tank crew were crouching behind it as well. One of them told me that the others inside were either dead or wounded so I decided to investigate. I was very wary about doing this as we were being fired on by machine guns and the 88mm, which, although it could not penetrate the two sides of the tank, was very unpleasant nevertheless. Our mortar men were going ahead with firing with their remaining shells. Anyway I thought I would take a chance. I tied my handkerchief to a stick or something and held it up in the air then climbed onto the tank and stood up in full view of everyone and to my great relief all the firing stopped immediately. I looked down inside the tank and saw a man obviously badly burnt sitting upright. I put my hand down to try to pull him out but all the skin on his wrist came away and I was pretty sure that he was dead – even if he had not been I could never have extricated him. I had a morphine injector with me so I injected that into his arm in case he was in any pain. I then stood up, turned towards the enemy and, to acknowledge their chivalrous temporary cease fire, saluted and then I climbed down off the tank top. As soon as I descended, taking my handkerchief down with me, all the shooting began again!

Not only did the firing begin, but also the enemy had worked out that they could only get to us by indirect fire and so brought their mortars to bear on our position. Using these, they could lob shells very steeply over the protecting tank and this they proceeded to do. Once again I thought that caution was the better part of valour. I noticed that there was an overrun trench about 100 metres away so I lined up everyone behind our tank and told them that when I counted to three they must run like hell towards the trench – by all of us going at the same time we could probably get there before the enemy realized what was happening. The plan worked and we arrived safely. We had to stay for some hours – until nightfall, but managed to survive until then when we all returned to the safety of our own lines.

The next night two of us decided to go out and try to find McGarity's body. This we did, with great difficulty, as there were bodies, Italians, and ours all over the place. Eventually we found him and tried to give him a decent burial. This was not easy because, although we had brought a pick and shovel, the ground was very hard and what made it even riskier, was the fact the enemy were not far away, so close in fact that we could hear them talking.

A day or two later the CO said that orders had come through that the bn. must put in another attack and clear the whole defensive position. Bertie Herbert, in command of the 'D' company, and another company, both greatly reduced in size on account of the casualties suffered in the first attack, would carry out the assault together. That night the CO told me to go with him when he went forward to give these orders. We found our way to Bertie's HQ which was in a very elaborate dugout constructed by the Italians previously – they had also left their stock of wines there, so he was living in enviable comfort – compared to ours back at bn. HQ. The attack was to go in just after midnight. After the orders had been issued Bertie was asked if he had any questions and I never forgot his reply which was in the form of questions – the answers to which he was well aware. He asked, "Approximately what was strength of the enemy in front" I gave the reply that it was thought that there were still about 300 – 500. He then asked, "On what front will the attack be launched?" and I was again told by the CO to give the answer (gleaned from Situation Reports which I was responsible for), I replied about 500 metres. Then Bertie said, "So I am to attack 500 of the enemy in well dug in trenches on a front of 500 metres with about 90 men?" the CO answered that those were the orders. Bertie nodded and after that we left him to prepare for the attack. But before we left I caught his eye and I could see that he knew that was the end for him. The attack duly went in and hardly any headway was made but also Bertie never returned. Later with some more fresh troops and the morally weakened enemy, the position was taken. Then we found Bertie's body way ahead of the line of advance – I gathered that after we had left him that night, he had partaken freely of his acquired stock of wines. When the time came for him to give the order to rise up and advance he strode off into the night, carrying his boy-scout pole regardless of the rest of the men, never to be seen alive again.

As a matter of interest I mentioned earlier that, on the route to this attack I had sent a couple of my men off to one side to ascertain whether the enemy were close by or not and they never returned. After this battle was won and the entire position captured these men were released from a temporary prisoners' camp. After I had sent them off they stumbled in to the enemy perimeter minefield. They sat still in it for the rest of the night and at dawn the Italians, seeing them there, shouted to them to surrender. The Italians were pretty rough with them, not giving them food and beating them over the heads. Eventually they were handed over to the German section to safeguard and here they received fair treatment.

One night we heard some bombers coming towards us and they started to drop their bombs and continued to do so for four or five hours. I was sitting with the CO in our dugout and, unthinkingly, started to whistle *Men of Harlech* which is similar (?) to the tune of the German national anthem. The CO was not amused, saying that it was bad enough being bombed by them without me whistling their bloody anthem! The next morning we listened to the news broadcast and understood that our Fleet Air had carried out successful bombing raids on the retreating enemy! It is worth noting that not many casualties were inflicted by our bombers as we were all well underground.

It was at about this time that I, consciously or unconsciously, decided never to wear a tin hat or my identity discs around my neck – a practice I continued to observe throughout the war. My headgear was the usual officer's peaked cap or, in the cold weather and at night, the short army scarf turned inside out and worn as a 'caps comforter'. My thinking was that to do so, would be to encourage the likelihood of damage to my head or, worse still, be found as a corpse and therefore needing to be identified! Fortunately neither eventuality occurred – perhaps I was just lucky.

The advance into the Cyrenaica region of Libya continued with the rest of 4th Div. (plus the Australians) rolling up the enemy along the coastline including the ports of Derna and Tobruk. We, the 7th Brigade, cut across towards Barce where we spent Christmas1942. The next morning the Brigadier sent me off in my little jeep, (I was now acting as a liaison officer in the HQ) to see what was going on in the large port of Benghazi. When I reached the outskirts of the town I entered very gingerly as I had no idea what to expect – were the Italians still there? Was the populace going to be friendly? I got down as far as the port promenade with no incidence so I drove the length of the dockside – still with no adverse reaction. Obviously the Italians had departed entirely. I returned to the Brigade which then came into the town and occupied it.

Chapter 8 : 1942

Western Desert Campaign, Retreat From Benghazi

While these operations in Cyrenaica were taking place, further to the West, in Libya, the Germans were reinforcing the Italians with the Panzer Division (Tanks) and an infantry division (The 90th Light). More important, they had a new commander (Rommel) who was to become very famous for his drive and military qualities – incidentally he was made to commit suicide by Hitler as a suspected conspirator in an assassination attempt against him. Rommel wasted no time in drawing up plans to regain all the territory lost before Christmas. His objective was to cut off all our forces in Cyrenaica. His first step was to advance to the south at Agedabia with his panzer division, then sweep up to the north heading for Tobruk. Our Brigadier (Harold Briggs) in Benghazi, heard of this move and gave the 4/16th PR the job of getting out to the north of the town and halting any moves that Rommel might make in the direction of the town, or trying to cut it off from the rest of the Division. I was back with my bn. at this stage and navigating the column out. It was raining pretty hard. Then we were fired on by what turned out to be the Germans who had beaten us to the exit route. Shortly after this discovery an officer from the brigade arrived telling me to report to the Brigadier. So I struggled back past all the congested traffic and found the Brigade staff all packed and ready to go. The Brigadier told me that he had decided to try breaking out of Benghazi, (which was now surrounded) in three columns one of which would be the Brigade HQ plus the uncommitted portion of the 4/16, a battery from the artillery regiment and any other ancillary units.

He told me that the route would take us south and then east, in so doing cut across Rommel's lines of communication – something he reckoned Rommel would not be expecting. He turned out to be quite right in this assumption. My job was to navigate this column. We set off from the centre of the town and headed for the southern section where there was known to be a gap in the minefield/perimeter. When I got to the gap – no one knew whether it had been mined by anyone – the Italians or our engineers. There was nothing for it but to find out the hard way – and soon. First of all I went along the gap on my hands and knees feeling for mines then, not having discovered any, I piled sandbags into the bottom of a truck, particularly around the pedals and drove slowly through in the wild hope that there would be no mines or, if there were, they would be of the Egyptian Pattern type which were not as explosive as our other types. Having driven through and back and nothing having exploded it was deemed to be safe and the column then passed through to the other side. Having got there the Brigadier had calculated that all the vehicles would not have enough petrol to reach our destination, some 300 miles away, so we drained the tanks and saved the petrol then vandalised the vehicles as much as possible – making them unserviceable to the enemy. I had 'acquired' a rather nice, but small, Fiat car in Benghazi and was sorry to have to get rid of it now.

Anyway, that done we set off in the pitch dark with me shining my torch backwards to guide the way for the following vehicles. During the night we passed a Bedouin village and heard all their dogs barking. When dawn came we spread out in the usual desert open formation (to make it more difficult for aircraft to damage us) and on I pressed. After an hour or so the Brigadier came up alongside my truck and said that the gunners had told him that I should turn the column towards the east. Immediately I demurred. While in Benghazi I had indulged in my hobby of roaming the countryside or desert and memorizing all slightly prominent features. One of them was a slight rise from the otherwise flat desert and this had, a long time ago, been some sort of habitation as there was an old Roman Bir (well) thereabouts. It had a name – Msus.

The gunners were adamant that we should go in that direction. I was not at all keen, as I had read a situation report the previous day, to the effect that Rommel's tanks were occupying Msus. The gunners were senior to me and so the Brigadier took their advice and they took over the navigation position in front. I was so sure I was right that I asked the Brigadier if I could take up a position out of harm's way and well away to the right of the convoy. He agreed. And so, on the column went again but now heading straight for Msus. When we got to within a mile or so of this high ground, suddenly three tanks appeared in a hull down position on the horizon. That was enough for everyone and, after much hand waving in my direction, I was recalled to carry on as before with my vehicle leading with its Blue Flag erected on the side. I turned the column back towards to the south again and after a short while arrived at a point near the much used track leading south from Msus. At this moment a motorcycle and side car started chugging towards us so I stopped and let him pass. I think he looked as surprised as I did but nothing was said or done and then he was gone. On we went all day, (unknown to me then, the three tanks had swept down on the tail of the column and nipped off the last three or four troop carriers, taking the men prisoners). I was very tired, not having slept for many hours and had trouble in keeping my eyes open to read the compass, so I got a man to stand behind me in the truck and to bang me on the head every time I dozed off. The following day we were still rumbling on at about 10 mph when I spotted some vehicles far away to the front. Not knowing who or what they were I stopped the column and proceeded very slowly. They too were very cagey. So I inched forward – so did they! I could see that they were armoured cars. In the end they raced forward to where I was waiting and they turned out to be from the South African armoured brigade. They escorted us thereafter towards Tobruk, and that was the end, more or less, of the 2nd desert campaign as far as I was concerned anyway. Rommel pushed our forces back and back to what became the Alamein Line. But that did not concern me and is another episode.

After the Brigade evacuated Benghazi, the 4/16th Punjabis were left behind to stall the German advance. However, when it became clear that resistance was not an option the CO called up his remaining officers and HQ staff and told them that they were free to try and escape as best as they could. What happened after that I don't know, but three officers, Richard McKinley, Ted Waite, 'Charlie' Chase and also the head clerk faded into the night heading east. The rest of the bn., including the CO and Adjutant were taken prisoners – including my Subedar Daim Khan. These three officers did eventually make the long and hazardous journey – some three hundred miles back to our lines where they rejoined us. Apparently they had been befriended by Bedouins who looked after them and helped them on their way – their camels passed on their ticks as well! The head Clerk (a Muslim like the Bedouins) settled down in a Bedouin village and stayed with them for many months. Our LRDG (Long Range Desert Group) visited him on a number of occasions and suggested that he was of more use there than back with us – for, by posing as a Bedouin, he could find out what was going on in the rear areas of the German advance. With his help raids were carried out on, amongst other places, airfields where a number of parked planes were wrecked. When, after Alamein, the bn. was moving westwards towards Tripolitania and passing fairly close to Benghazi our Head Clerk asked if he could go and find the Bedouin villagers with whom he had stayed. Sure enough he found them and the Headman presented the officers' mess with a small goat, which was immediately called 'Rastus', why I don't know. He became famous for the terrible smell he generated. Even when he was shaven and an army blanket converted into a coat for him his smell lingered on. Rastus stayed with the bn. travelling through Egypt, Palestine, Italy and back to India, smelling all the way! He was with us for many years but his story is quite a long one and not too relevant to my memoirs, even though the goat became very attached to me and always tried to butt me if I was anywhere nearby. When I did leave the bn., there was no one to stand by him and he was put down – poor old Rastus!

Chapter 9 : 1942

After Benghazi, To Egypt, Palestine

After the retreat from Benghazi we had to reorganise the bn. more than somewhat, as half of it had been captured in that town, including the CO, the Adjutant, the Quartermaster, most of one rifle company and the HQ company including our clerks and all the filing systems. And last but by no means least we had lost all our followers. Let me explain. All Indian regiments had about 40-plus followers attached to them. These men were not soldiers and not subject to military discipline. They did the things that the soldiers would not do, for example all the cooking, the sweeping and cleaning out of the lavatories, ablutions and, believe it or not, every sepoy would be shaved each morning by one of the *nais* (or barbers). The most junior would be shaved very, very early and the more senior much later. Without these men life was not too tolerable for the Indian sepoy.

When we got back to the Delta we were stationed in a camp outside Alexandria and from there we used to make regular and frequent forays to the fleshpots therein. A lot of heavy drinking took place here and five of us formed a drinking team and challenged all-comers in a well-regulated competition. We had no trouble in finding any opposition as all the drinks were on us! We were never beaten, but had a drawn match against a Naval team from the minesweeper squadron in Alex. Whilst here, we received a new CO – the last having been taken prisoner as I have said. This new chap had never heard a shot fired in anger and was just not geared to active service conditions and he certainly did not know how to deal with us 'older' but much younger hands than he. He had a hard a time. Shortly after he arrived the bn. was required to send an officer to a new venture of the 4th Ind. Div. The plan was to have a training school especially to train men in the art of patrolling – both reconnaissance and fighting types. I was the reconnaissance instructor. This school was to be situated at a site in

Palestine (Israel), between the Sea of Galilee and the coast. We were allowed to sustain quite a percentage of casualties in the interests of real life patrolling. I was detailed off for this job as the Urdu-speaking instructor; there was also a Ghurkha-speaking officer and two from English regiments, plus an RE (engineer). This course was only a temporary scheme to while away the time until the Division would be called on again for operations. It became well known and all sorts of men were sent to attend it: men from other Divisions, e.g. the New Zealand, the Australians and even the Greek Brigade. It fell to my lot also, to organize the officers' mess and the troops' canteen (NAAFI). No sooner had we started than I had complaints from the sergeants' mess saying that their beer was awful – having tasted it myself I had to agree so I called for the contractor and told him to rectify the matter. The beer was apparently locally brewed from potatoes. When I went to my tent that evening I found a bottle of whisky and 100 cigarettes waiting for me, no note but I knew whom it was from. I drank the whisky and smoked the cigarettes. Two days later the sergeants complained again so I called the contractor and he was most upset and asked me if had got the gifts – I agreed I had and thanked him very much but said the beer must be changed. That night I found two bottles of whisky on my bed and 500 cigarettes that I shared out with some of my friends. Next day I got the same complaint and once again I sent for the contractor and he was even more upset. That night the officers' mess went up in flames and all our stocks went with it. This was followed by a visit from the contractor who asked for compensation for all his stores and equipment.

As this was not an official organization I did not think that I could get any money from Army sources and would have to pay up from my own funds. I knew the contractor must be at the bottom of this disaster but could not prove it. His charge was quite exorbitant and so I tried to get him to reduce it but he would not budge. There were two officers of the Royal Sussex on this course, one always carried a revolver slung very low with a bandolier of bullets across his chest and the other always looked rather sinister in his overcoat with a turned up astrakhan collar (incidentally when the latter was killed at Cassino it came out that he was a baron knight of the realm!). One day I asked these two to accompany me on a mission. We went into Haifa and I barged into the contractor's office by myself, but unannounced. I had left the other two just outside. Once again I asked him to reduce his charge, again he refused so I called in my two ‘heavies’ who sauntered in menacingly. The one leaned right over the desk while the other started playing around with his revolver – pointing it at the contractor. I then asked him again to reduce the charges, which he promptly did. I gave him a cheque and got a receipt as having been paid in full. The beer was changed as well!

The sequel to this event was that a year or so later, after the Monte Cassino battle I was in our Brigade HQ mess tent and having a drink(s) with the officers (including the Brigadier) and I recounted this story. At the end of the narrative he turned round and told his (DAQMG) to reimburse me for the full amount I had paid the contractor!

Chapter 10 : 1943

Cyprus

In the Mediterranean the Germans had captured Crete by using airborne troops and it was thought that their next stop would be Cyprus, so 7th Brig. was sent over there. Obviously, there were not enough troops, so we all had to pretend we were larger units than we actually were – the brigade became a division, Bns became brigades, companies became bns. I doubt if this fooled anyone. It was also decided to site and dig dummy bn. positions around the island. I was given this job and had to go round on a motorbike dealing with the villages – getting their help and, where necessary, paying them.

When I was not doing this I was partying in the capital, Nicosia with my friends and regret to say that we got into rather a lot of trouble. So much so, that the CO 'confined us to barracks' regularly. Of the four or five months in Cyprus, four of us must have spent most of our time confined.

We had a very pleasant time in this island, which, in those days, had not been commercialised at all, and we were more or less on peacetime duties. We started off camped outside Nicosia in a place then known as the Yaraloukas Magazine. It was quite close to the town so we had no difficulty in getting in and out – and we did that very often! There were a number of bars and cabarets, the latter with girls and artistes all of whom were from the various Balkan states. In theory we were not allowed to fraternize with them, nor be seen sitting with them, however we got over this rather stupid obstacle by sitting on bar stools which the house would arrange in a line along the bar then we and the girls would sit on alternate stools.

One day we were informed that the Prime Minister of the Punjab (Sir Sikander Hyat Khan) would be coming to visit the bn., which by now had been moved to a campsite outside Larnaca. The day before his coming, five or six of us went into town (with me driving the truck) to have our usual jollifications; this party included our adjutant, Lewin Tugwell (whom I will refer to again at a later date – in Tunisia). When I reckoned everyone had had enough I shepherded them back to the truck and they all piled in – except the adjutant. He just would not get in so I led him round to the open back of the truck and pointed up to the bright moon – he looked up and I gave him an upper cut and knocked him out – then put him into the truck and we went back to barracks. The next morning of course, there was a parade for our VIP. None of the officers were able to make it, not even the adjutant whose job it was to take the parade, so I was detailed to 'carry on' – this was not too easy, as I had not taken part in the practices. The parade went off all right, however everyone, including myself, was confined to barracks again.

Finally, we were brought back to Egypt where our forces had been driven back by Rommel to the Alamein line. We tarried awhile in the Delta area by what is euphemistically called the "sweet water canal" where the mosquitoes were enormous and I think I got bitten by one. From there we went to the Mena Camp, near the pyramids and we again had too much of a good time in Cairo and yet again were gated by the CO. I must admit that we did give him a very difficult time but I don't think he was really up to the business of command. He was a good administrative officer with great knowledge of rules and regulations and a great help in sorting things out, after our having lost so much at Benghazi, but he could have done things differently. I believe he went back to India and was made commandant of a prisoner of war camp, which I'm sure he did very well. Finally we were called forward to take over a part of the Alamein Line.

Chapter 11 : 1943

Back to the Western Desert, Battle of Alamein

In 1943 the bn. went up and rejoined the 7th Brig. on the Ruweisat Ridge, which was in the central section of the Alamein line. This defensive line extended from the coast to the north, then south through and over Ruweisat Ridge which was, in fact more of a hump than a ridge and was about 40 metres higher than the surrounding desert. From there it ran south again to the sea of sand at the Siwa oasis. The day before we actually arrived on the site the CO was called forward, to be told by the brigadier where the bn. was to take up its position. He was obviously not quite sure of himself in a real life battle area and so, much against his will I imagine, he asked me to accompany him. I sat next to him during the briefing and took notes.

Afterwards, when we went to our area, he was quite out of his depth looking at this desolate featureless terrain and told me to get on with it and draw up a plan. This I did and we returned to bring the bn. up. We then settled in. Time passed and I carried out night patrols. The desert was too open to do much in daylight. Our lines were about 1000 metres from the enemy minefields. In between was no man's land, which was strewn with derelict tanks and vehicles – the aftermath of various battles.

The CO had an idea that I should go and do a short attachment to the Australians who were dug into the sides of the Tel-el-Eisa (meaning 'Hill of Jesus') railway cutting to the north of Ruweisat. When I got there I went and introduced myself to the company commander who was sitting in his dugout that was carved out of the side of this four-metre high cutting. He wondered what I was there for, so I told him I had come to learn how they did their night patrolling.

EIGHTH ARMY

Personal Message from the ARMY COMMANDER

1—When I assumed command of the Eighth Army I said that the mandate was to destroy ROMMEL and his Army, and that it would be done as soon as we were ready.

2—We are ready NOW.

The battle which is now about to begin will be one of the decisive battles of history. It will be the turning point of the war. The eyes of the whole world will be on us, watching anxiously which way the battle will swing.

We can give them their answer at once, "It will swing our way."

3—We have first-class equipment; good tanks; good anti-tank guns; plenty of artillery and plenty of ammunition; and we are backed up by the finest air striking force in the world.

All that is necessary is that each one of us, every officer and man, should enter this battle with the determination to see it through—to fight and to kill—and finally, to win.

If we all do this there can be only one result—together we will hit the enemy for "six," right out of North Africa.

4—The sooner we win this battle, which will be the turning point of this war, the sooner we shall all get back home to our families.

5—Therefore, let every officer and man enter the battle with a stout heart, and with the determination to do his duty so long as he has breath in his body.

AND LET NO MAN SURRENDER SO LONG AS HE IS UNWOUNDED AND CAN FIGHT.

Let us all pray that "the Lord mighty in battle" will give us the victory.

B. L. MONTGOMERY,

Lieutenant-General, G.O.C.-in-C., Eighth Army.

MIDDLE EAST FORCES,
23-10-42.

Order of the Day.

He wasn't too happy about this saying, quite rightly, that the moon was too high and bright at that time so I sat around for a couple of days in the cutting dugout I was allotted. It was two metres high with a corrugated roof and the doorway was just a blanket hanging down from a crossbeam. They were a good crowd. The lavatory was two seats; side by side out in the open in between the railway lines! Then it happened. In August Rommel had decided to make one final assault to take Cairo which entailed breaking the Alamein Line and, in particular, through the Australian defences and more in particular, along the Tel-el-Eisa cutting. The assault started with the usual heavy artillery bombardment, which went on all night. I just sat there, with nothing to do. Not having any responsibilities, I settled down with a bottle of whisky. The noise was terrific and I gathered next morning that the German infantry attacked right up to our positions but were stopped from getting any further. When I went outside I discovered that a shell must have hit my doorway, as it was no longer there – just a broken crossbeam. I had slept through it all. Even the double lavatory seat had been smashed. I decided that I was not serving any useful purpose so I returned to my bn. and company on the Ruweisat Ridge.

One night I went out on a patrol with a Jemadar and two men. The idea was to find out something about the enemy minefields. I set off at midnight and when I got to a derelict tank in the middle of no man's land I left the two sepoys there with orders to stay until I got back or to return to our lines at 4 o'clock if I did not return. I then went on with the Jemadar. I always preferred operating on my own; you only have yourself to blame if anything goes wrong. Additionally I could move very quietly – when I was alone. We two got to our side of the suspected minefield, which was only marked by a cable – not the usual barbed wire fence. I indicated to the Jemadar to stay put and that I was going on alone. We could hear many Italian voices in front of us and all the time they were obviously very jittery for they kept firing Very lights up, parachute flares to light up the area. When this happened I lay very still until the flares landed and were extinguished, then crawled on a bit more, feeling for any anti-personnel mines.

I had planned to get into their lines but suddenly I saw a man about twenty metres away from me. He seemed to be watching me so I lay still and watched him. After a while I thought I saw him turn towards me and raise a weapon. That was enough, so I made a quick decision to take a chance on the minefield rather than being shot at close range. I jumped up and sprinted back the way I had come – I saw this other man doing much the same but on a parallel line to my flight. When I got some way out of this minefield (fortunately I did not set anything off in my flight) I slowed down and heard the Italians shouting behind me. Then I made my way back to the tank to pick up the sepoys, but they had gone. I went back in their return direction and soon heard them in front of me, whispering to each other, so I thought I would play a joke on them. I went quietly and quickly round and passed them, and then I lay in wait. When they got near I accosted them in what I thought was guttural German but I was wasting my time because they recognized my voice and answered me in Urdu!

When I got back to my lines I reported that what had happened and was told that the Jemadar had already returned with a slightly different story. It turned out that when I went on alone he, not wanting to be left out of anything, followed and he was therefore, the man I saw. When he saw me run off he did the same. I was very, very cross with him as all sorts of things could have happened as a result of him disobeying my instructions.

One day the CO asked if he could come out on a patrol with me – I think he only wanted to say that he had patrolled in no man's land. I was not too keen as there is no cover in the desert. Anyway we went a few hundred yards – I pretending that we were achieving great things but keeping our heads well down. Then I developed an awful headache – this had been troubling me for some days in the latter part of each day. I said I must return and when we re-entered our lines I collapsed and didn't come round for some days, and then in an army hospital on the Suez Canal. I was recovering from a severe bout of malaria. In the bed next to me was a Southern Rhodesian magistrate who had joined up on the outbreak of war and was then serving in one of their artillery units situated just south of the Ruweisat Ridge. When we recovered from the very debilitating effects of the malaria we were told that we would have to go to a convalescence camp to get our strength back. At that time everyone knew that the desert army, now renamed the 8th Army under Montgomery, was going to launch a big offensive against the Afrika Corps under Rommel in the near future, so we decided that we would run away and rejoin our units. One night we packed our few belongings and crept out of the hospital. We managed to hitch a lift to Cairo and then onto the Indian Reinforcement Camp at Mena. On arrival there, I was given the bad news that I had been posted as being AWOL (absent without leave) that is a polite way of saying – a deserter!

The good news was, that at the Camp I met our new CO, the other one having been relieved of his command as being incompetent. The new CO had been sent a car to collect him and to take him up to Alamein; this suited me very well and the Southern Rhodesia officer asked if he could come along for the drive. When we reached our position at Alamein the Rhodesian asked to be taken on to his unit and dropped off there.

A week or so later I thought I would go and visit him, as we had become good friends. When I got to his unit I got the bad news that on the very day he arrived back and rejoined his battery the German artillery had decided to carry out counter-battery fire and one shell landed on his guns and he was killed.

D-Day for the Alamein advance was fixed for 9.30p.m., Friday 23 October 1943. Prior to that, hundreds of guns had been brought up closer to the front line so that they could bring down counter-battery fire on the German artillery and also, of course, on the German defence positions, thereby ensuring that they kept their heads down while our infantry advanced. I won't go into this battle as we, in the 4th Ind. Div. did not play a large part in it. In fact our job was to protect the left flank of the main attack. When the barrage started, it was the biggest artillery barrage ever to have been launched at that time – we got out of our trenches and watched in safety and comfort though, being not too far in front of the gun positions. It was very noisy indeed. The attack lasted 12 days, at the end of which the breakthrough came and the armoured divisions charged forward rolling up the enemy lines.

The 4th Ind. Div. passed through the now open minefields and followed the retreating Italian/German armies through to the Mareth line on the frontier in between Tunisia and Libya.

Chapter 12 : 1943

Tunisia, Mareth Line (Matmata Hills)

While the rest of the 8th Army was mopping up in Libya and Cyrenaica, chasing the retreating Afrika Corps towards Tripoli, we in the 4th Div. followed up until we reached the frontier between Tunisia and Libya where the Mareth Line was situated. This line of defences was originally fortified (pre-war) by the French but now occupied by Rommel's forces.

After the Alamein battle, the 4th Ind. Div. moved westwards (in transport) as stated above, towards Tripoli and Tunisia. On one occasion we were spread out in the normal open desert formation when some Luftwaffe Messerschmits decided to strafe our convoy. As usual we all got out of our transport and dispersed left and right. I was kneeling and watching the progress of the planes when, looking round, I saw one which seemed to be homing in on me. I saw it coming in low and straight for me firing away with guns blazing and kicking up spurts of bullets making a channel about 4 metres wide – and I was kneeling in between these two lines of fire. There was nothing I could do about it but just stay still and hope that I would not be hit. I was right – I wasn't. The planes flew away and we all then carried on as before.

This Mareth line extended from the sea southwards to a range of hills called Matmata. We took up a waiting position and sent out patrols. One day, a newly arrived officer, Ronnie Glynn, was sent out on a night patrol – his first, and with troops who did not know him. When he was out there, he heard a noise and stopped to look and listen. He thought he saw an enemy patrol and decided he would attack it. He got up and went quietly back to his men (only four of them) to tell them his plan of action. They promptly got up as well and retreated hurriedly to base, leaving the officer behind. He hung around a while then he too returned. On arrival back he understood that they had reported him as missing and probably taken prisoner.

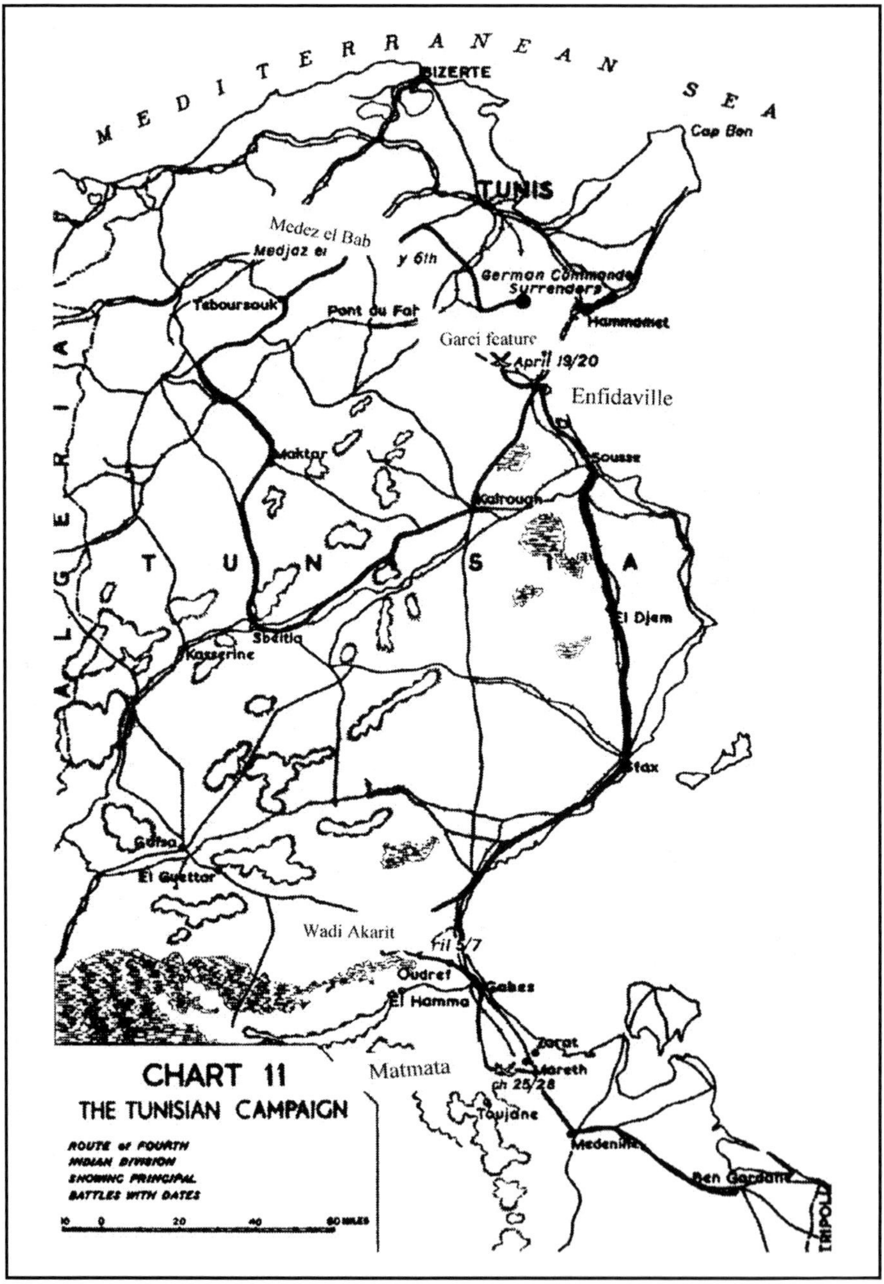

Map of Tunisia

I did not know anything about all this, as men from my company were not involved. Later that night I got a telephone call from the CO to go and see him. He told me to get a firing squad together and, in the morning, to shoot the men for cowardice and deserting their officer. I asked for time to investigate and talk to the men concerned. I knew the Havildar (Sgt.) concerned and he was a good man. He said that they did not understand what the officer was up to, and when they saw him coming back they thought he was retreating so they did likewise. However, they should not have left him on his own and I really rubbed this in to them. As to the shooting party, the CO accepted the explanation and I gave a sigh of relief at having got out of that situation.

The next night, or it might been a later one, in view of what had happened above, I decided to send a patrol out to more or less the same area, as the enemy obviously were patrolling it themselves. A young Indian officer had been with me for a couple of months so I detailed him to take a party of about eight men out just to listen and report if there were any further signs of the enemy – nothing more. They were to set off at about midnight and I went along to see them off from our lines. When I got there, my Subedar and a couple of other men from the company were also present. Then this officer turned to these three men and myself and started to say goodbye as if he was never going to see us again. This, in front of the patrol he was taking out! I immediately took him to one side and told him to return to his tent and that I would take the patrol instead. The next morning he was sent away from the bn. and back to Cairo and possibly India. This may seem unfair in retrospect but, in a warlike situation with men's lives at stake, you cannot have doubts creeping into the men's minds. They must be sure that their officers are confident in what they are doing. For the record I did not see or hear anything while I was out that night.

While we were hanging about, before the assault that was being planned I, and other company commanders from the Division who would be taking part in the forthcoming attack on the Mareth Line, were told to go right back to General Montgomery's HQ – to meet the great man. It was a foul day with rain pouring down – I remember it only too well. When I eventually got to the HQ I found about eight other officers waiting there. We waited in the rain until Monty emerged from his famous battlewagon.

He came up to us, shook us by the hand, said not a word then retraced his footsteps to the battlewagon. I believe that was what he considered as ‘getting to know’ his men!

I personally, was not impressed.

When the main assault started our Brigade filtered though the hills. The 4/16th was travelling along a narrow winding road. It was pitch dark and we halted. I was called forward to the CO’s car and he said that the other (5th) Brigade on our right was pushing the enemy back and their brigadier wanted someone to cut across behind the enemy line of retreat and to cut them off by straddling the escape route. I was told to do this – there was a problem here, as it was thought that the retreating enemy had probably mined the roadsides. With this thought in mind, I obtained a long strip of white material and tied it to the belt at my back then I set off on my hands and knees across the suspected area – crawling my way very gingerly and feeling the ground for mines. My company followed keeping close to the white tape that was trailing behind me. After 70 metres I reckoned it was safe to proceed upright and we carried on until, just before dawn, I hit the road and strung my company across to await the arrival of the retreating enemy. They never turned up, so presumably they had all retreated earlier in the night. This episode stood me in good stead some years later, for that brigadier became the Director of Military Training in GHQ, India. I had need to obtain a recommendation to re-attend the Staff College, Quetta and he was just the man to give it to me!

From the Mareth line the 8th Army then chased the Afrika Corps up through Tunisia until it reached what was to become the battle of Wadi Akarit. The main attack was to be delivered from the centre of Tunisia towards the sea. The 4th Div. was to take the hilly ground overlooking the battle area and so deny observation for the enemy’s artillery.

Our brigade, the 7th Ind. Brig., was to make a night attack on the enemy’s positions in the hills to the east of the road.

Chapter 13 : 1943

Tunisia, Wadi Akarit

In or about 1 April 1943 we, the 7th Brigade were settled down just south of Wadi Akarit awaiting the next phase of the campaign. I and Capt Popple (commanding 'A' Company) were sent for by our CO (Lt-Col Hughes) and told to carry out a reconnaissance patrol to the hills immediately to the west of the road (Gabes-Gafsa) that runs south to north at a point where the road enters the hills. The object was to ascertain whether there were any enemy positions to the west of the road. The patrol was to be carried out that very night. At about midnight we set off with two sepoys. After we had travelled three or four hundred metres or so we decided to drop off the sepoys and go on by ourselves as two people would make much less noise than four. We went on very slowly for about two hundred metres when we heard voices to our front. We reached a point where there was a small valley running northwards so we inched our way up this valley and I could hear Italians talking amongst themselves. It was very dark and we could not see anything, so, not wanting to risk walking into them, we turned back and returned to the two men we had dropped off and then back to our lines before dawn. All we had established was that there some enemy positions west of the road.

A few days later we were called to bn. HQ and given orders/plans for the Division and Brigade part in the forthcoming 8th Army attack on the Wadi Akarit defensive position which spread from the road and Fatnassa Mountains down to the sea. The 4th Ind. Div. would deal with the mountains on the left then the 50th Div in the centre, with the 51st Highland Div. on the right, the 4th Armoured Brig. (of the Desert Rats) pushing through any gap that was breached.

The main army attack was scheduled for the morning of the 5th April but the 4th Ind. Div. was given the task of putting in a night attack onto the hills of the Fatnassa feature – hopefully to capture the high points and denying these to the enemy artillery observations posts who could have directed artillery fire onto the main offensive which would be taking place out in the open plains below.

The plan was that the brigade would form up just after dark. The Brig. would be packed tight with every man just able to see the others to the front and two sides. So – with certain ancillary troops such as Sappers, Medics, gunner ops, machine gunners etc. this large body must have exceeded 2500 men – all advancing into the pitch dark for a silent attack.

After some time the Ghurkhas were sent off followed by the Royal Sussex. Our bn. waited for the Brigadier ('OZ' Lovett) to send us off too. Then we heard noises to the front and realised the Ghurkhas must have got stuck into the enemy at their objective, but the noise was not overmuch considering what was taking place. Then in the darkness, a runner came to me from our CO and I went to receive my orders. Although it was very dark one could see the silhouette of a line of hills to my front and left but for all I knew they could have been 100 or even 1000 metres away. Anyway my orders were to advance with my company and take the hills.

I went back to my where my men were kneeling and waiting. I gave the platoon commanders similar orders. I said when they saw me stand up and move forward they should do the same. Having given them time to pass on my orders I rose and started forwards but then something happened that I was not prepared for. Instead of advancing steadily and silently forward they all rose and started to charge meanwhile yelling their war cry, "Maro, Maro Hadri – Maro, Maro Hadri" at the top of their voices. There was no chance of me now stopping them so I joined them charging even faster than them and got in front. Soon I felt the terrain rising until I reached the top of what I presumed was my objective. There was a certain amount of small arms fire but no casualties at this point as far I could ascertain. I spread out my men along this ridge and waited for the dawn.

As the early dawn light came up I soon realized that there was another ridge to my front and the enemy was on this in some force. I called up the platoon commanders and told them we would be putting in an attack as soon as possible. The enemy position to my front was about 150 metres away across a shallow valley. My orders were very simple. When I got up everyone else must do so as well and with, bayonets fixed, we would charge forward in line yelling our heads off in the process.

It was all over quite soon, I charged forward with my signaller beside me. He was carrying a wireless set on his back. About halfway across the intervening space he was hit and fell, however I went on with my men until we reached this ridge behind which the enemy were sheltering and firing at us. As soon as we reached the top of the ridge they held their hands up to surrender. The nearest one to me was a tall officer and I was very cross as he, or they, had shot my signaller. I was sorely tempted to shoot this officer there and then – I think he thought so too. Anyway, I didn't, but I told him to turn around. Behind this defensive ridge was a steep drop of about 30 metres, so I gave him a great big kick, which sent him hurtling down the slope. When he reached the bottom I shouted to him to run back up again.

On arrival back, very puffed, I told him to get all his men out and onto our side of the ridge. By now the enemy gunners had realized that their forward line here been taken and, as is normal practice, started to shell it. The Italian prisoners were now in a state of abject terror. A medical officer of theirs came and told that me that he had a small dressing station (with wounded men) just below this ridge and asked me to send some of my men to go and bring the wounded up and out of the gunfire. I indicated to him that there were many of his men there, cowering as low as possible, and that he could use some of them for this rather risky job. There were no volunteers! And thereafter I lost interest in his plight.

All these prisoners were Italians – except one who was a German *feldwebel* (corporal), probably a gunner op. He could speak a little English and as we chatted, enemy shells were dropping all around us – I was not going to let him see that I was afraid, and obviously he had the same thoughts as I, however the shell fire did eventually stop and so, with a sigh of relief, I returned to the business in hand.

Meanwhile I was receiving a certain amount of small arms fire from a steep hill across the road, to the west. So I sent a platoon under Havildar Mohd Aslam to cross the road behind this hill and then to attack the enemy entrenched there. While he did this we fired everything we had to support his advance. When his platoon reached about halfway up behind the Italians, they had obviously had enough and waving white flags and handkerchiefs, they clambered across the uneven terrain towards me, joined their comrades and were ready to march off in surrender under a 'guard' of three or four of my men!

In all, this attack had produced over five hundred prisoners. From where I was standing I could see that all the terrain to my front, and the road, as far as Point 275 was clear of enemy. I reported this to bn. HQ in the hope that higher command would exploit this advantage by sending the tanks through. It was very early morning, and the main battle had hardly begun in the plains. I still hold the view that had the armour been sent through and behind the Fatnassa Mountains it could have decimated their gun positions, taken many prisoners and, what's more, reduced the number of casualties inflicted on our attacking troops. But that is the opinion of a junior officer. Incidentally, my signaller recovered from his wounds. I was awarded the MC for this action and on my recommendation the Havildar got the IDSM.

Chapter 14 : 1943

Tunisia, Djebel Garci and Enfidaville, The Garci Feature

After the Wadi Akarit battle the 7th Brig. moved further up north and then came up against more defensive positions in the region between the Djebel Garci hills and Enfidaville on the coast. The bn. was told to occupy the foothills. The brigade wanted to know something about the terrain to the front and whether tanks could be used. I was consigned for this patrol job. In particular to find whether one dry riverbed, which was pointed out to me on the map, was tank proof – also there were many enemy positions sited around that. I decided to go and have a distant look at the land by daylight. A British company held the front line there. I arrived and asked to see the company commander and my informant, a private, told me with a funny look in his eyes that he was "over there". I went 'there' and found this officer cowering behind a dry riverbank. He was in no state to help me and demanded that I leave his company area, as my presence would probably bring down enemy gunfire on him. I returned to base and reported this incident to the Brigade Major. This chap was removed and sent back to the Delta – he was, in my opinion, a menace to his men. The next night (at 3a.m.), I went out from this spot with two sepoys. After I had covered about three hundred metres I discovered a small, well camouflaged, hidey-hole obviously used as an observation post – by their gunners? There was a telephone cable leading up to it so I dragged that along with me for a distance then cut it up. On I went until I heard sounds in front, so I left my two men there to wait until I returned. I went forwards very slowly and found myself at the edge of the reported riverbed. It was too dark to see it properly but I'm sure it was very deep and impassable to tanks – another deterrent to climbing down into it was the fact I could clearly hear German voices on the other side, so I turned away towards the west where could I also hear voices, but the terrain was flatter and I could move very quietly and did so, for I nearly trod on a German sentry. He must have been as surprised as I was for he quietly said, *"Achtung"*, probably not realising I was not 'one of his' and tried to stop me falling into his trench. I made a quick decision and walked off even more slowly, hoping that he would keep on wondering who had nearly fallen onto him. This delay enabled me to reach a fold in the ground some fifty or so metres away, in which I then lay down. I did not have long to wait. Obviously the sentry had discussed what he had seen and there then followed a stream of machine-gun fire, which fortunately passed over my head. I hung on there for half an hour or so and returned to my two men and thence back to our lines to report what I had seen and heard.

A day or so later the bn. was ordered to occupy and consolidate the hills (also known as the Garci feature) to our front. As I was not involved in this assault I was able to watch it from a distance. This is when we first came across a new German weapon – the *nebelwerfer*. This consisted of six or eight barrels fixed together, all electronically connected. The shells were very large containers of high explosive that went off on contact with the ground. These containers were inserted down the barrels and were electrically fired off together. When they hit the ground – they did so in clusters – the explosion was quite frightening itself but, worse still, the casing of the shells fragmented into very large chunks and could do a lot of damage to a person. As these projectiles flew through the air, they travelled quite slowly, emitting a high-pitched whining sound and this was likened to a 'gaggle of geese'. The bn. had to cross an open plain to get to the hills and the enemy OPs easily spotted their advance. Consequently a hail of nebelwerfer shells came down on them. As I say I personally was not involved in this advance but watched in great admiration from a distance – no one broke ranks nor was the advance halted at all and the bn. reached and clambered up the rising ground.

My turn came the next day. I was called up on the wireless and told to come up with my company and not only to join the bn., which had got as far as a valley and there had been held up by too heavy fire, but I was to go on even further up the valley and take the top end. By this time the enemy was more than ready for us. We advanced in open order and then everything seemed to be brought to bear on us. I looked to the side of valley and saw the CO and adjutant there in shallow trenches. They were waving at me to go on and then, as I was watching, a shell landed and burst on the side of the adjutant's (Lewen Tugwell) trench and he was severely wounded, but did live to see another day. (I digress now. This adjutant, whom I knew well, later married, had two children but when he was about 50 years old he changed his sex and became a woman! As I say I knew him very well then and much later too – after the war. He never ever gave any indication that he was anything but what he was – a regular British Amy Officer – Sandhurst trained! When he recovered from his severe wounds and on the demise of the Indian Army he was transferred to a British Army artillery unit and went off and fought in the Korean War).

When I arrived at the top of the valley – how I shall never know, as the shells were dropping around me like rainwater, we sort of settled down as best we could. We did not have any picks and shovels, only our small trenching tools, which were quite useless in the very rocky ground; we could only scrape indentations and pull rocks around the edges. And there we sat for about a day and a half – I really cannot remember for how long, but I was completely dazed from the pounding we were subjected to. We were told to retire and so fell back to our original position in the plains below. When we got back I went to our mess tent – ordered one drink and passed out on the floor until the next morning. It was the only time in the whole war that I felt shell-shocked – absolutely numbed. I was woken up to be told that the CO wanted to see me. He told me that we would be moving to an area north of Enfidaville and take over from a Guards bn. I was to go and size up the area and make arrangements with the Guards' CO on the take/hand over.

I could have done without this job, as I was still a bit numb from the Garci feature. However I set off in my jeep with a driver. We passed through Enfidaville and went north where I was stopped by an MP (Military Policeman) who warned me that the road in front was in full view of the enemy artillery OPs who, when they saw a vehicle driving along it, brought down fire on it. I asked him what was the best thing I could do and his laconic reply was that I should drive like hell. With this advice still ringing in my ears I sped off, reached the end of this 'mad mile' safely and searched around the olive groves for the Guard's HQ. As I approached it a shell came winging its way towards me and hit the front wheel of the jeep severely wounding my driver but I escaped unhurt. The irate Guard's CO shouted at me to get the hell out of his immediate area, so I moved over about fifty metres and sat down with my back to an old olive tree, when another shell arrived and struck it. Fortunately it was a dud and did not explode but it did split the tree right down to the ground. Again I escaped scot-free. I managed to get the Guards to organize my return to my bn.

A couple of days later we moved and took over from the Guards in the olive groves NW of Enfidaville. In front of us were some British troops of a division recently out from the UK and new to any form of warfare. Two days later we saw lots of them retreating rapidly back through the olive groves – shouting to us to get back too as the Germans were attacking. Fortunately our men stood fast and let them pass through and after a while all was well and peaceful again.

Opposite our position was a long craggy ridge on which the Germans had formed a formidable defensive line with minefields protecting their front; they also had a searchlight trained on the minefield which, at night, was switched on every now and again (I never did realize why our artillery could not or did not put that light out of action!) This line in front went under the name of the Tebagga feature. One day there was a CO's conference at which he told us that the bn. had been given the task of attacking and capturing that feature. My company and one other were told to carry out the attack the next night. I took a quick glance at the other officer, (Geoffrey Popple) and we looked at each other, but the unspoken word was that we knew we did not have a hope in hell of succeeding and that that would be the end of us. During the day we two crept forward to see the terrain in daylight, and we did not like what we saw.

Soon after nightfall while we were preparing ourselves, we were very relieved to be told that the attack had been called off. The relief was short lived for the next morning the attack was 'on' for that night. Again, after nightfall, the operation was called off. This time for good. The reason being that the 4th Ind. Div. had been paired off with the 7th Armoured Div., and that we were to swing round to left and join the 1st Army (which had been advancing from Algeria along the north African coast and which was experiencing trouble in the capture of Tunis.) The move round was quite a feat in itself, as it had to be carried out with hardly any notice, secretly, and at night with no lights and very poor roads. For one division it would have been difficult but for two (one armoured), it was well nigh impossible. But we did it in one night. All our transport had been well used over in the desert and been held together with string, metaphorically speaking, no lights etc. etc. and we had travelled right the way across North Africa from Egypt some thousands of miles away.

In the early morning we stopped at the small township of Le Kef and there were some British troops of the 1st Army there – all in new uniforms, and new vehicles. Some of our Royal Sussex soldiers leaned out of the trucks and asked the British 1st Army troops if it was true that they had got chocolates and English cigarettes in their rations and the reply was, "Yes, but you've got to earn them first!" That started it. The Royal Sussex boys piled out of their trucks and got stuck into these 1st Army types, causing a lot of damage and even more grief until it quietened down and our column continued on its northward journey to Medjez-el-bab.

Chapter 15 : 1943

Medjez-el-bab, To Tunis

I don't remember too much about what happened next – it was over 50 years ago! We met up in open ground behind the battle area-to-be. All the company commanders who were going to be involved got together with the tank commanders. Montgomery only agreed to 'lend' his two best divisions to the 1st Army, on condition that all the planning and the command rested with him.

The G-o-C of the 1st Army (which was comparatively fresh out from the UK) was there and he was appalled how we 8th Army officers were attired – corduroys, cravats, shorts and all sorts of hats and suede leather desert boots, e.g. I was wearing a pair of chocolate-coloured corduroy trousers. When this G-o-C remarked on these divergences from correct dress our Div. Commander told him that if any two officers were dressed the same – one would have to go!

The battle plan (for a change taking place in daylight) was that two brigades would separate into companies and the companies would, with the tanks in support, punch a hole into the enemy defence line, each company leap-frogging over the one in front. In front of the advancing troops the artillery would lay a creeping barrage that would make the enemy keep their heads down and behind which we would closely follow. My company was the last one of all in this leap-frogging game so I watched what was going on – moving forward all the time until my turn came. My objective was a piece of rising and fairly open ground. I could not see any enemy but could see their trenches. When we got nearer the enemy position I called out for the charge, with fixed bayonets, and the men ran forward yelling their usual battle war cry. When we got to the top there was no one was there – they had all retreated but, as usual, the enemy's gunners then started to bring down artillery fire on their old positions which, of course, were now ours!

I, and my men, took cover behind and under our supporting tanks and felt much safer. I was looking around when I spotted our CO who had come forward to assess the situation. He was right out in the open so I called to him to come and join me under my tank, He came running up and lay down beside me. Then a shell must have hit the side of the tank, ricocheted along the side, hit something, perhaps a nut or bolt and went into the CO's leg above the knee. There was a lot of blood so we used his lanyard and put on a tourniquet , called up his jeep and away he went – out of the war. He refused to have his leg amputated back at the hospital but had to have a contraption of springs to move his feet and ankles – for the rest of his life. That didn't do him much harm for I believe he went on to become Deputy Lord Lieutenant of Wiltshire and also MFH (!) of their hunt.

After this operation we split up, the brigades going off after the retreating enemy. I went roaming off in a southerly direction and, rounding a bend in the road, came upon a mass of enemy. I advanced cautiously in my jeep not knowing what to do but as they seemed not to be aggressive I went on to be greeted in a very friendly manner by a bunch of senior officers. All they wanted to know was where they should go in order to surrender. I sent the whole lot of them, probably about 2000, off on foot, unguarded. The next evening I went into Tunis to join in the celebrations and they were pretty riotous. About 1 a.m. an orderly came from bn. HQ to the hotel in which I was celebrating (how he knew where I was I shall never know) and told me that I had to report back to bn. HQ. On arrival the CO told me that I had to leave immediately, pick up another officer from the Ghurkhas and travel post-haste to Tripoli – that night! That was the end of my (and the 4th Indian Div.) war in North Africa.

Chapter 16 : 1943

Post Tunis, Egypt, Training Team, Lebanon

As I have already said I was sent back to the Delta, via Tripoli; At Tripoli we were then told that we were to go back to the Delta and join a training team!

The flight back was not without incidence. After about an hour (there were only four of us on the small plane), we noticed a lot of smoke coming out of the starboard engine. We told the pilot and he made a steep emergency landing on an airstrip at Benghazi. The trouble was rectified and we continued the flight to Cairo. On arrival there we were whisked off to a site near the Suez Canal. Here we were told what it was all about. During the war, up to this date, the garrison troops on Malta had been isolated. It consisted of a brigade of British troops. They had to be trained in warfare and particularly patrolling. Our team consisted of a Brigadier and five other officers. We were given about three weeks to complete this assignment – not long!

Before we had finished this training the news filtered through to us that this 'Maltese Brigade' was to be the spearhead for landings in Sicily. On completion of the training there was to be a practice landing and exercise up the Gulf of Aquaba and we, the training team, were to go as umpires. We all embarked and sailed up the Gulf to what is now the thriving tourist resort of Eliat. In those days it consisted merely of a few fishermen's mud huts. The night landing went off, not without incidence I might add, and I would not have felt very confident of a successful outcome myself. However they were very successful when it came to the real thing on the Sicilian beaches. After this exercise was over, the news came through that the ships, and the brigade, were to go straight up the Suez Canal and on to the landing proper in Sicily. In the interests of secrecy the training team was to go with them. Consternation! Our brigadier managed to get a message right across North Africa to our Division HQ in Tunis and there in turn, our Div. Commander managed to have our inclusion in the landings cancelled but only on the condition that we were confined to a hotel in Cairo, and not to leave it at all until the landings had taken place and become general knowledge. So we were stuck in this hotel – a not too severe confinement! I imagine we were so confined for about 6 – 7 days and then we returned to our units.

Eventually the Division and the 4/16th returned to the Delta and from there the Brigade was sent to Tripoli (in Syria) to practise mountain warfare. This wasn't taken too seriously and it involved many parties in the Tripoli town itself.

This might be a good place to refer back to Jack De Manio.

I mentioned that I met Jack, first of all, in Eritrea. His bn. was involved in an attack, the details of which I know nothing. He gained his MC here and also was wounded. He was sent back there to be evacuated to a hospital in Egypt. He recovered there and eventually rejoined the Royal Sussex.

He was a commissioned officer in the Territorial Army before World War 2 and joined up as soon as war was declared. He was a remarkable man and popular with both officers and men. He was a company commander most of the time that I knew him. He had one big fault in that he could not live within his means (pay) and tended to overspend. I really don't think that he had a dishonest thought in his head but when his funds ran low he would 'borrow' from his company funds. As I understand it, he was married to a wealthy American woman (in the UK) to whom he would turn, now and again, and she would send him the wherewithal to repay his 'loans'. He was not a womaniser as such, but when there were girls present they would flock around him, like flies around a piece of meat, he just had that something that the rest of us lacked – in his presence! For instance when we were in the hills behind Tripoli (Syria) doing mountain warfare exercises, four or five of us went into Tripoli to party in the bars/cabarets – wearing regulation uniform, of course. We went into one cabaret and sat down at a table. We saw Jack there – not in uniform, but wearing a very stylish riding habit and jodhpurs; he had been out riding somewhere. As usual he was hemmed in by girls but not for long as no doubt, he was running out of money because he soon came across and joined us. After a while I saw two or three of the girls going round the tables with a hat and asking for 'money for the band'. We all dutifully subscribed. When the girls had completed their rounds they came over to our table and laid the hatfuls of money down in front of Jack! I must say that he was very 'generous' with his new found wealth and stood drinks all round until the money was all gone. He was well known in the Division for his money manipulations but no one seemed to care because, as I say, he was a very amiable character. However the CO of his bn., at this time was, I believe, promoted and another commanding officer sent to replace him. At this same time his bn. was lacking a PRI (President of the Regimental Institute) and this new CO put Jack in charge. A PRI's job is primarily concerned with running the regimental funds and accounts. When news of this appointment got about there was an audible gasp around the division as the outcome was a foregone conclusion. Sure enough Jack started ‘borrowing’ money but when the time came for him to straighten the accounts out he, as usual, turned to his matrimonial ‘banker’ in the UK. But this time she said, enough was enough, and refused to ‘sub’ him any more. The result was he was sent for a Court Martial.

One of our officers (Jimmy McCarthy) went sick and was admitted to a hospital in Haifa (I think it was). He was in a ward one day when who should walk in but Jack De Manio. He was awaiting his Court Martial but looking around he told Jimmy that he rather liked the look of this and the nurses and said he would also get himself admitted; sure enough a couple of days later he walked in and the ward sister directed him to a bed next to Jimmy. When the ward sister had left, Jimmy asked him on what grounds he had himself admitted and he said he was suffering from piles. A couple of days later another officer was wheeled in on a stretcher having been operated on. After an hour or so this man came round from his anaesthetic and he looked very poorly. They asked him what operation he had undergone. His answer was on the lines of: “phew”, “ouch”, “ooh” “oh, oh, oh,” “never again” etc. then went on to tell them he had just had an operation for piles. That was enough for Jack; he dressed quickly and discharged himself without further ado!

At his Court Martial he lost his commission and was reduced to the ranks and sent to a Transport unit. On his first day he went to the notice board to see what duties he had been allocated and read that Recruit De Manio had such and such a duty. He asked to see the commanding officer, said that as he had a number of years service to his credit he should be not be addressed as a recruit but as a private. His CO agreed and said that he would put that right. The next day Jack went again to the notice board and read that Private De Manio was on such and such a duty. He again asked to see his CO but this time he pointed out that he should have his MC decoration inserted after his name. He was quite right because this had not been taken away from him at the Court Martial. I would point out that Military Crosses are not awarded to other ranks so his name and MC on the 'orders' board was quite unique. I lost track of him after this but I understand that as he was bilingual (English and French) he somehow got himself a job on the Forces radio programme based in the Middle East. The war ended and the years rolled by. Then a new name came on the BBC early morning 7a.m. and 8a.m. chat show – one Jack De Manio. He became a household name and was listened to far and wide. His talks would cover day-to-day topical items, which he conveyed with his normal casual style. Unfortunately he rather over did it on occasions and was not oversensitive whom he sometimes ridiculed. The BBC was not so easygoing in those days and eventually they took him off. When he asked if he would be allowed to attend the 4th Indian Division Officers' Association Dinners in London (an annual event) no one objected at all and on the odd occasion, when he was passing by Camberley in Surrey, he would pop in to see me.

At the end of this mountain warfare training – preparatory to our future task in Italy – the bn. was sent down to Haifa there to await further orders. The CO. decided that he would not travel with the bn. but would make a detour seeing the countryside including Damascus. He suggested that I accompany him, which I was only too willing to do! We visited the Cedars of Lebanon and Baalbeck on the way to Damascus. When we arrived there it was to discover that a curfew had been imposed on the town – especially for Army personnel. We were talking, and bemoaning our lot, to the manager of the hotel where we had stopped for the night and he suggested that we go into the town incognito wearing some of his civilian clothes – trilby hat included!

Before we left the hotel he sprayed us with some very strong-smelling scent – I don't know where he thought we would be visiting! We went to the 'Street called Straight' and there saw some of the night workers in metal workshops, glass blowing, food stalls etc. then we were enticed into a large emporium containing all sorts of goods. The owner eventually sold us some things. I personally bought three Damascene inlay trinket boxes that fitted into each other and also a large tablecloth. Then the tricky question of how to pay for them arose, as we had no local currency. The owner had no worries on this score and asked me to write the amount on a slip of paper and address it to the manager of the Ottoman Bank, in Cairo where I happened to hold an account. He, on his part, was to dispatch the articles to my mother in India.

He trusted us, even though we were not in uniform and must have looked pretty shady characters in our borrowed clothes! Anyway my mother got the goods and he got his money. It is sad to say that such trust doesn't exist nowadays as everyone has to be able to prove one's integrity and financial status before anything can be bought on credit and goods parted with. The next day we continued our journey and rejoined the bn. in Haifa.

Chapter 17 : 1943 – 1944

Journey to Italy, Hospital

From our campsite near Haifa we embarked for Italy in late December 1943. I was promoted to the rank of major. I was 24 years of age.

We arrived at the port of Toranto and from there went up to a small village called Auletta, which has an old castle belonging to the Duke of Aosta. We settled down in various buildings around the village – my company took over the village school and I had a small room in it, which leaked very badly. The officers' mess was in the castle itself that, by the way, had a fine old drawbridge over the moat.

We spent a very, very merry white Christmas there with deep snow all around. We knew we would be required to carry out attacks across the rivers that run down to the sea all the way up the east coast of Italy – so, in order to get my men used to this, I laid on a practice river-crossing for my company. We would wade across a river, do an attack on an imaginary enemy position on the other side then sit in a defensive post for a few hours in our soaking wet and icy clothes. Ice was floating down the river and both banks were covered in snow. It was extremely cold. When this exercise was over we returned to our billets in the village.

I immediately fell ill and in no time was almost unconscious with fever, sinus and whatever – running a high temperature. The MO arranged for me to be taken, by ambulance, to the nearest hospital at a town called Potenza. On the way the ambulance was stopped by snowfalls across the road and we had to come back and try again a couple of days later. I was really poorly by this time. While I was in hospital the brigade had continued on up the east coast to confront the enemy who were dug into defensive positions in the area between the hills and the Adriatic Sea.

Map of Italy

The civilian hospital in Potenza had been taken over by the army; it had pretty basic facilities with just holes in the floor for the loos and the single bathroom doubled up as a wood and coal store.

Some time previous to this the army nursing service had changed from what it used to be: a change I thought rather sad. Prior to the changes the service went under the name of The QAIMNS (Queen Alexandra's Institute of Military Nursing Service). There were two 'ranks': Sister wearing two pips on her shoulder and Matron wearing a Crown on hers. All ranks in the army, generals and privates included, would salute these nursing sisters whenever they were met. They wore white or grey dresses with a scarlet cape – very distinctive and easily recognizable. After the change they were given army ranks of Lieutenant, Captain, Major etc. and now of course they had to salute officers senior to them and the other ranks had to salute them – a very sad and retrograde step in my opinion.

In the bed next to mine was another officer from the 4 Ind. Div. the Light AA regiment. We got on well together and when we were told that, before being discharged, we would have to go and spend some time at a convalescence depot at Sorrento this did not suit us. He had kept his personal vehicle and driver, somewhere in Potenza. One night, when we felt strong enough, we crept out of the hospital and drove off through the night, towards somewhere north of Bari.

The next morning, we were driving along a main road and suddenly saw vehicles coming towards us bearing the 4 Ind. Div. Red Eagle signs. I inquired where the 4/16 PR were and was told that they were just behind. When they came up, I stopped a lorry carrying my company's men and hopped on board. I was back 'home'! I might not have been quite so happy had I known that the Div. and bn. was on its way to a place called – Monte Cassino! I recall that we were held up in the plains near Venafro, waiting to go to the Cassino positions held by the American 34th Division. The poor roads were very icy causing the vehicles to slide all over the place and into each other.

Chapter 18 : 1944

Monte Cassino Battle

The 7th Brigade was ordered to take over from the Americans who had taken up positions in the hills north of the monastery. On or about 13 Feb. the bn. had to cross the Liri valley in order to reach the foothills to the north of the monastery. As the valley was in full view of the enemy guns, the journey of about three kilometres had to be carried out on foot at night. Just at the foothills, I found myself in a destroyed Italian cemetery – one of those surrounded by thick walls having burial compartments built into the walls. Some of them had lost the front panels. As we had to wait there for the rest of the night I told my men to rest up until dawn when we would finish our advance – out of sight of enemy 'eyes'. I settled down and spent the rest of the night in one of these empty graves.

On reaching these foothills our bn. was ordered up to take over the position captured and occupied by the Americans 34th US (Mexican?) division overlooking the monastery to the north. They had suffered terrible casualties and I, with my company (I was Company Commander of our Punjabi Mussulman company) was to take over from what was left of a battalion of Americans – 600 men reduced to just about 40!

When the CO told the American brigadier (who was a sick man) that an attack was going to be made on the monastery, but not until it had been bombed, he woke up and said words to the effect of "Jeeze – if it is incumbent arn you to depend on our barmers of the USAAF, and I wuz in your shoes, waal I'd hie me back to dear old Pittsburgh". After that less than encouraging prognostication we went forward to take over our allotted tasks.

We moved up to our position at night. It was very cold and snow was all around. We had to do it all very quietly as the Germans were only about 30 metres away on the top of the hill (Point 445) under which we going to crouch for next 7 weeks. We could hear them talking – and no doubt, they us! As the crow flies the monastery was only some 200 metres away.

Personal Message from the Army Commander

Great events lie ahead of us. All round Hitler's Germany, the Allies are closing in: on the East, the victorious Russians drive on — in the West, the British and American Armies are massed to invade.

— Now in the South, the Eighth and Fifth Armies are about to strike.

Side by side with our French and American Allies, we will break through the enemy's winter line and start our great advance Northwards. Our plan is worked out in every detail — we attack in great strength, with large numbers of tanks and guns, supported by a powerful American Air Force and our own Desert Air Force.

The peoples of the United Nations will be watching the Eighth Army. Let us live up to our great traditions and give them news of fresh achievements — great news such as they expect from this Army.

We welcome gladly to our ranks those Divisions whose first fight this is with the Eighth Army. We send a special message to our Polish Corps, now battling beside us to regain its beloved country.

I say to you all — Into action, with the light of battle in your eyes. Let every man do his duty throughout the fight and the Day is ours!

Good Luck and God Speed to each one of you!

Lieut.-General.

ITALY,
MAY, 1944.

Order of the Day.

We could not move about during the day as the German positions to our right overlooked us. Movement during the night was not too safe either as the Germans had machine guns trained on our area on 'fixed lines' along which they would fire when they felt like it, even though they could not see us of course. Our food was brought up at night. It was the responsibility of my quartermaster havildar to bring the food up to us. One night he set out with three men but he never arrived – not that night anyway, so we had no food at all that day. What had happened was that in the pitch darkness, he had slipped left past my position and crept forward unwittingly around behind the enemy position in front of me and down into the valley leading up to the monastery. He then heard movement in front of him so he, and his party, froze. The Germans brought up a mortar, set their guns down and proceeded to fire into our lines – albeit the rear ones. He didn't dare move but sat partially hidden until eventually, before dawn, the Germans withdrew. However, by this time he couldn't move because of the daylight so he stayed there all day – any movement and he would have been spotted. That was not the end of this, or of his problems, because our bombers came over that morning and bombed the monastery, only one hundred or so metres away! He stuck it out until nightfall then quietly retraced his footsteps and we then got our rations – a day late!

Talking about food – then, and on many other similar occasions, I would eat the same rations as my men. 'Hard scale' rations, necessary when cooking facilities were not available, usually consisted of a curry mix, which was folded into chapattis. Fortunately I was then, and am still, partial to Indian food.

From a vantage and safe point I could see the Germans taking their wounded into a doorway at the bottom of a high wall of the monastery building – presumably this was the First Aid post. They would put up a red or white flag and everyone would stop firing until they pulled it down again – we did the same to carry our wounded back to our First Aid post.

When I took over from the Americans, their commander told me not to bury any of their dead – and they were all around (probably well over 50 in number) so we had to put up with that – not too pleasant, as the bodies were disintegrating but, due to the cold, there was little or no stench – nor flies for that matter. But they did breed lice. And I acquired plenty of them. I could not get rid of them from my clothes for many weeks after we got out, in fact sometime in May.

A couple of days after moving into position we were told that the monastery (and Cassino town) were going to be bombed by the USAAF (Flying Fortresses) and that, as I was so close to the monastery, my position would be inside the bombline and I would get nearly as much as the Germans – and I did! They came over in fifteen waves and took all the morning to drop their cargo of bombs. Each aircraft was probably about 100 feet (30 metres wide) and they kept a distance of, say 200 metres between each aircraft. They came over in waves, 12 abreast so they were strung out over distance of more than a mile wide. The centre of their target area was the town and monastery in front of me. We could only sit it out as they kept coming over and over – inevitably we sustained many casualties. This was all repeated some weeks later with another bombardment along the same lines.

One day I had a very lucky escape. From a vantage point behind a low stone boundary wall and looking across a field, I saw two Germans moving along the far side about seventy metres away. I slowly raised myself up, quickly took aim and got them both. I then got down quickly, but only just in time for, unbeknown to me a German sniper to my left had spotted me and fired, hitting the branches above where my head had been.

The day after the bombing, a curious thing happened. I was looking over the same wall bordering the field in front of me when I saw, walking across the field, an old woman and a child. I did not hail them to come over towards me as I thought the Germans might have sent them purposely in order to see where they finished up. They eventually reached the wall a bit to my right and once they had come down out of sight I indicated to them to come and join me. The old woman and the little girl were, understandably, in a state of shock and very frightened. With some hand sign language I gathered they came from a farm, just the other side of the field and had been there while all the bombing was taking place. I kept them with me until nightfall then sent them back to our bn .HQ.

A few days after the first bombing the CO got on to me and said that I might well be asked to put in an attack and capture the Point 445 which overlooked my position and on which the Germans had defensive posts. I recall saying that I thought I could do this – probably with some

Above : Royal Military College, Sandhurst, new buildings (C 1935).

Right : Self in ceremonial uniform, RMC Sandhurst (1939).

Officers of the 4/16th Punjab Regiment in the Western Desert (1943).
The author is third from right in the back row.

Malay Regiment ceremonial dress uniform (1953).
Self with Malay Officer and my CSM and CQMS.

Above : Relaxing in my jungle hammock on operations in Malaya (1953).

Left : Self returning by boat from a jungle operation. A dead Chinese communist terrorist (CT) is wrapped up beside me!

Normal dress uniform, Malay (1951).

success, but followed this up by stating I would then find myself, and my men, on the forward slopes completely overlooked by the Germans on the high ground to my right and even more so by their positions in the ruins of the monastery to my front. I considered that we would be obliterated within the hour after dawn. I heard no more on this subject and suppose the CO had passed on my views to the Brigadier. A few days later I was told that an attack was going to be launched by the Ghurkha bn. but a little further along to the right of the Point 445 feature. This was going to take place the following night. As the attack was to pass very close to my position I was ordered to move all my men to one side so there would be no danger of a mix up. Now, I knew that the line of attack to my right was almost impassable due to the steepness of the terrain, the large rocky outcrops, the thick undergrowth and the Germans' positions. Once while wandering/crawling to that area I came face to face with a German – only a few yards from my right-hand post. We both faded away backwards! I strongly suspected that he was placing anti-personnel or shoe mines down. Anyway, I honestly thought that this proposed attack was doomed to fail, so got on to my CO and asked if I could come back and speak to the Brigadier and CO of the Ghurkhas. I thought that the route I was going to use, had I carried out my attack, was much easier as it involved a left-hook over flatter terrain. But the CO said that it was too late for the plans to be changed. I rather suspect that my original hesitancy might not have been overpopular with the powers that be, and he therefore thought they should be left to get on with their plans.

That night I pulled my men back as instructed and eventually heard the Ghurkhas in the valley at the foot of the climb – then they began their charge up hill. There was much noise, bangs and small arms fire to my right but I could not see anything owing to the darkness. After a long while all was quiet once again and I was told, on my wireless set, that the attack had failed, the Ghurkhas had withdrawn, and my men and I returned to our original slit trenches. I was later to learn that all the company commanders had been killed, that there had been many, many casualties and the Ghurkhas' CO was seriously wounded. I understood that most of the casualties were caused by shoe and anti-personnel mines. The attack never even got as far as the German positions.

Soldiers of the Allied Armies in Italy

Throughout the past winter you have fought hard and valiantly and killed many Germans. Perhaps you are disappointed that we have not been able to advance faster and farther, but I and those who know, realize full well how magnificently you have fought amongst these almost insurmountable obstacles of rocky, trackless mountains, deep in snow, and in valleys blocked by rivers and mud, against a stubborn foe.

The results of these past months may not appear spectacular, but you have drawn into Italy and mauled many of the enemy's best divisions which he badly needed to stem the advance of the Russian Armies in the East. Hitler has admitted that his defeats in the East were largely due to the bitterness of the fighting and his losses in Italy. This, in itself, is a great achievement and you may well be as proud of yourselves as I am of you. You have gained the admiration of the world and the gratitude of our Russian Allies.

Today the bad times are behind us and tomorrow we can see victory ahead. Under the ever increasing blows of the air forces of the United Nations, which are mounting every day in intensity, the German war machine is beginning to crumble. The Allied armed forces are now assembling for the final battles on sea, on land, and in the air to crush the enemy once and for all. From the East and the West, from the North and the South, blows are about to fall which will result in the final destruction of the Nazis and bring freedom once again to Europe, and hasten peace for us all. To us in Italy, has been given the honour to strike the first blow.

We are going to destroy the German Armies in Italy. The fighting will be hard, bitter, and perhaps long, but you are warriors and soldiers of the highest order, who for more than a year have known only victory. You have courage, determination and skill. You will be supported by overwhelming air forces, and in guns and tanks we far outnumber the Germans. No Armies have ever entered battle before with a more just and righteous cause.

So with God's help and blessing, we take the field—confident of victory.

H.R. Alexander

General,
Commander - in - Chief,
Allied Armies in Italy

May, 1944

Order of the Day.

I won't go into the whole battle (because it has been well and better documented elsewhere), but it went on for many weeks with attacks being put in here and there – not one of them succeeding. But to cut a long story short, some months later the monastery fell to the Poles who had suffered terrible casualties (hadn't we all?), but the monastery, which had been defended by units of the German First Parachute and 15th Panzer Grenadier Divisions eventually fell more through being surrounded to the north and west by other armies. My company was in this forward position the whole time without any relief – non-stop for 7 weeks. As a matter of fact, and interest, I personally was "up there" probably longer than anyone else – other people were either killed, wounded, evacuated or relieved for various reasons. I went in with some 95 men and came out 7 weeks later with all that was left – 27 men – and that was after having received reinforcements to make up the numbers as they went down and down.

The Germans were using the high ground of the monastery as Ops (Observation Posts) and could see all that was going on in the open Liri River valley below and therefore could direct their artillery fire at will. To overcome this disadvantage our artillery put down a smoke screen onto the monastery so they were not able to observe what was going on below them. Fine – but, the monastery, and the hills around, funnelled all sorts of winds so the smoke screen had to be changed consistently throughout the day (and on moonlit nights) and very very often the wind came from behind my position so the gunners directed their smoke shells ON to my position from where the smoke then drifted over to the monastery thereby blinding the OPs. So for hours on end we received these shells into our lines – although they were not explosive it was most unpleasant to have these solid shells and their equally solid bases hurtling about the place. My very good friend, Popple, was hit by one of these base plates and had to be evacuated to hospital with a chunk out of one of his buttocks – he eventually was sent back to India.

At this point the CO decided that I should take over the command of Popple's Sikh company. So I waited until dark and then moved across to the right where I took over Popple's now empty dugout. The Germans were just as close here so there could be no movement in daylight. One just lay there all the time in this rather cramped space.

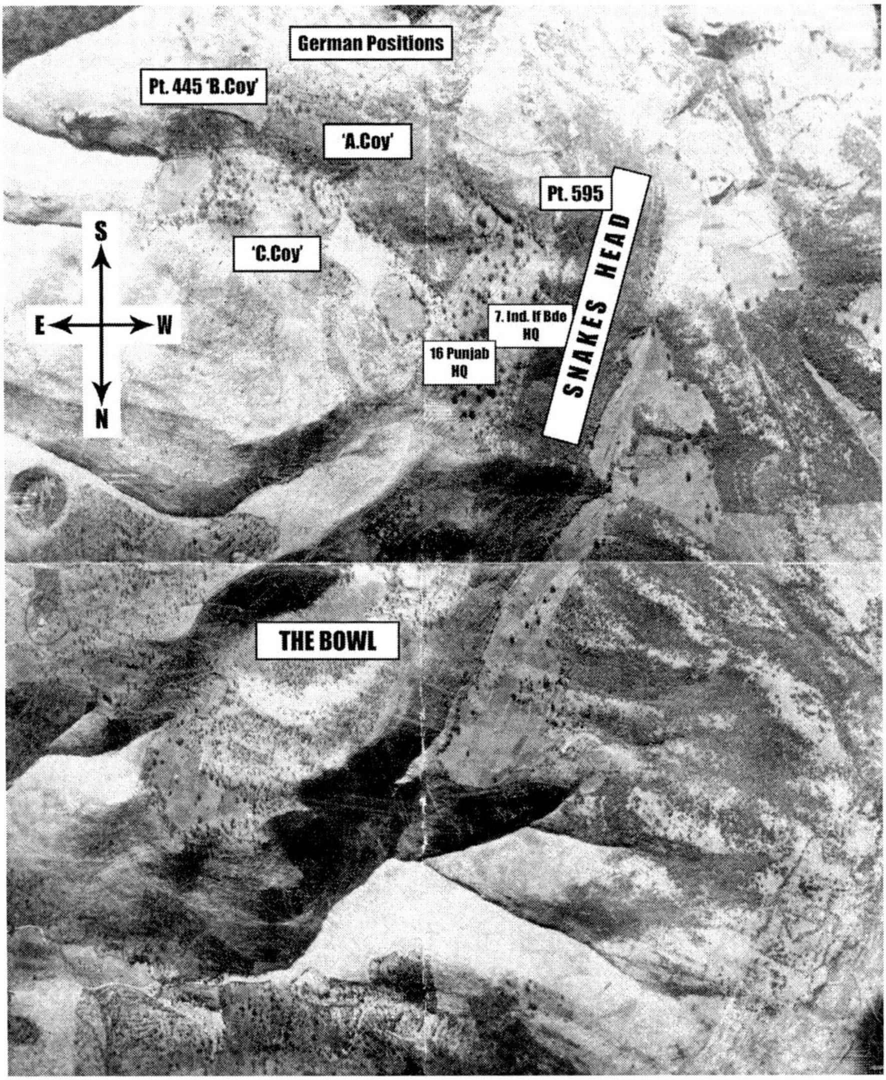

Aerial view of Monte Cassino battle.

When I changed over companies another very good friend of mine, Richard McKinley, who had been at Sandhurst with me, relieved me. He was an Irishman and a good soldier. When out of the line, and he had imbibed more than a few drinks he would rail against the British – much to the astonishment of the Indian officers present. He was a brave man, foolishly so. In the position I'd left, the Germans would either lob hand grenades down on to us, or small mortar bombs. Shortly after he took over from me this happened and he thought to make little of it to his men so he got out of his slit-trench and wandered nonchalantly around outside until one of these missiles landed at his feet and wounded him in the stomach very seriously. He was taken back to our First Aid post but died soon after.

Our bn. had a rear HQ in a comparatively safe place tucked into the foothills below. Here the rations and cooking facilities were organized by our recently joined Quartermaster – a Capt. Smith. I had only met him once. It was his great misfortune to find himself on the receiving end of an enemy barrage directed to the general area behind our forward lines and he was killed outright.

Where I was with the Sikhs the defensive position only covered an area of about 70 x 40 metres and, in this confined space, were lived out our lives in slit trenches about 2 metres long and 2 metres wide, over which we laid our groundsheets to keep off the snow/rain. Here too we could not move during the daylight hours and at night we had to be wary of not being caught in the line of the Germans' night time fixed lines machine gun fire. I would point out here that the sanitary conditions were non-existent; just behind my small position there was a shallow indentation in the ground and which was not visible to the enemy. And there we all went to relieve ourselves – as had the Americans before us so you can imagine what the conditions were like; fortunately, the rains and snow saved us from the inevitable smells.

Anything landing in our confined area was a 'close one'. Soon after I took over, we experienced early morning shelling by our artillery. In fact, it was aimed for the enemy on the other side of the Snakeshead high ridge to my right. Unfortunately, some of it landed in my area and so, on the wireless set, I complained, but the gunners tried to convince me that I must have been mixing up the enemy shelling with theirs. I suggested that a gunner officer should come and spend the night in my area and see for himself. Reluctantly this was agreed, and that night he came up and settled into a makeshift trench. Sure enough the next morning the shelling started as usual and he very rapidly called a ceasefire to his guns and then systematically got them to fire one by one until, by a process of elimination, a rogue gun was found to have changed its position and it was realigned –

to my great satisfaction. The CO sent another officer up to join me and to start with we shared my dugout. However, I don't think he liked it very much, especially my killing of the lice in my clothes with cigarettes. He had also been warned that anyone near me was very likely to be wounded. Some time later we were pulled back and were relieved by a Ghurkha bn. We only went back a short distance to a resting area, known as 'the bowl' where the next morning, five of us officers were standing around in a circle eating our breakfast, when a shell landed right in the middle of us – but fortunately it sank down into the mud and did not explode. A few minutes later I went off to one side and sat down with this young officer, and he was congratulating himself on having survived his attachment with me when yet another shell landed quite a distance off, say 70 or 80 metres away, but one piece of shrapnel flew through the air and lodged itself in his kneecap – this was not life threatening in itself, but he was evacuated and I never saw him again.

That night we heard some small arms firing taking place from the direction of my old position but thought nothing more about it as night firing, particularly on 'fixed lines', was a common occurrence. However a couple of hours or so later I was sent for to report to Brigade HQ where I was informed that the company commander who had taken over from me, had left his post saying that Germans had overrun him. Being a Ghurkha company, there were no British Officers left and I was told to go forward to find out what had happened and stay in command there until relieved. This was not too easy as I was not a Ghurkhali speaker, so I approached very warily. However, I met up with one of the Ghurkha VCOs and gleaned from him that when this officer heard the night firing on 'fixed lines' from such a close range he concluded that his position had been overrun and, without further investigation or concern for the rest of his men, he retired. I don't know what took place when he reported to Brig. HQ but he was not seen again. The following night, as promised, I was relieved and was thankful to return to own my men.

The day came at last for us to leave the Cassino hills, but as when we came, we could not move across the Liri valley in daylight. When the bn. did go off I was detailed to be the last to leave, and as it was too late for me to go that same night I stayed on a further day. When I did arrive back, the officers' mess tent had already been erected. I had some breakfast, then one glass of whisky, but that was enough, I immediately flaked out (as I had done after the Garci feature in Tunisia) until the next morning. I suppose this must be some sort of delayed reaction/relief but after that all was well again! Anyway I could now concentrate on getting rid of the lice!

Later I was told to go and talk to our Brigadier. After some humming and hawing and with some embarrassment he said that our bn. had been through so much, starting with the Eritrean campaign and all the desert campaigns and what would I feel about the bn. being taken out of the Division and being relieved by another comparatively fresh bn.? I myself was becoming a bit tired of front line soldiering and this was my answer on behalf of the men. There were only two officers left who had served non-stop from the beginning, 'John Henry' Knight and myself. I doubt if there were more than 20 or so other men in the bn. who could say the same. Another of the longest serving regiments, the 4/6th Rajputana Rifles, was also relieved.

In the Indian Army, a battalion had, if it was lucky, 8 to 10 English officers. At Cassino we lost two, killed, and had four wounded – in other words over 50%. When we did get out, the presence of lice was a common factor with all men, and the powers that be decided to send out disinfestations units. And this is how they decided to rid us of them. I am not sure of the exact numbers involved, but the gist of it was: A unit consisted of a large cabinet, say 2 metres long and 1 metre deep and into this the contaminated garments would be placed, together with a block of something that would kill the lice. Fine – but this cabinet could only hold, say, fifty garments to say nothing of bulky blankets and the disinfestations process ran on for about an hour. Fine again –provided that we could keep the unit for some days, but no – owing to the great demand, each Brigade was only allotted the unit for one day, consequently each Bn got it for half a day (or less) and so on. There was no possibility of doing all the contaminated clothing/blankets in the prescribed time so what happened? Each man was only allowed to insert one garment, so after he got that back, it joined the other still infested articles and he was back to square one. Compare that with the American system whereby a disinfestation tent was erected, the men divested themselves of all lice-ridden clothing and walked into another tent to be issued with a completely new set of everything!

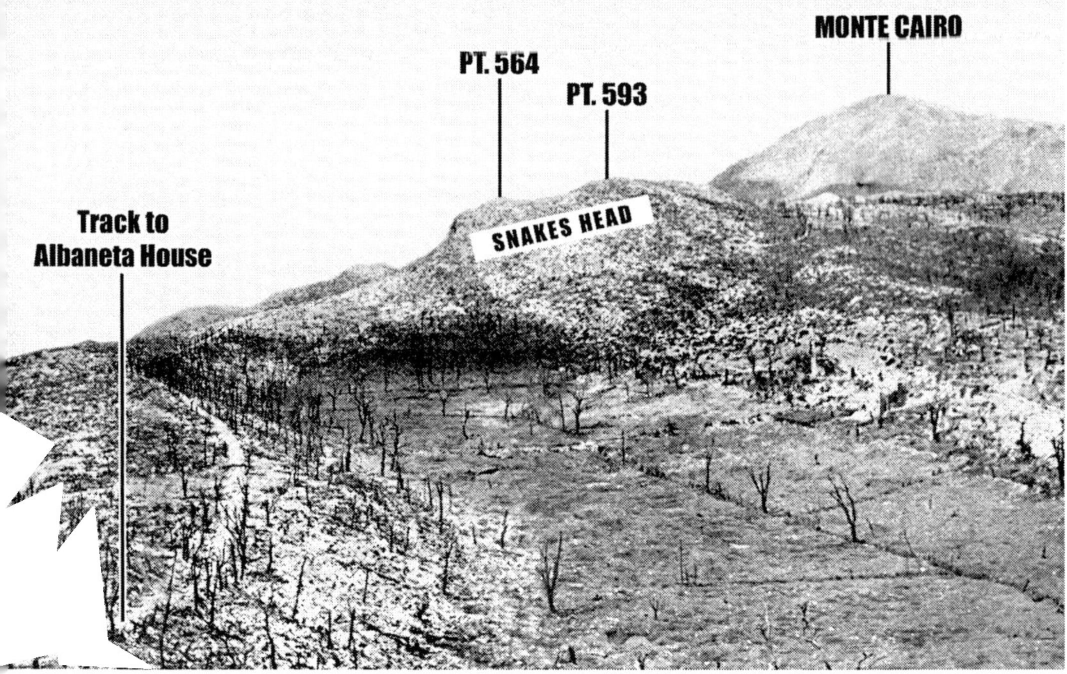

This view from the enemy occupied Monastery some 250 metres away with 'no mans land' between.

Cassino Monastery 1944. Photo taken from my 'A' Company forward position, 200 metres from the monastery walls.

Cassino Monastery after it was rebuilt in 1987.

Chapter 19 : 1944

After Cassino, East Coast Italy

After withdrawing from the Cassino campaign, the 4th Ind. Div. (which had sustained more than 4000 casualties) was sent over to the east coast of Italy where the Axis forces were holding a line in the area of Pescara. It was the task of the Division to push them back up north.

Before the bn. left the 4th Ind. Div., there was work to be done. When we got to this front the Germans opposite dropped leaflets onto the Division announcing that they were the same parachute troops (15th Parachute Division) who had given us a bloody nose at Cassino. They were indeed a very tough regiment and they too had suffered terrible casualties.

Again I am a bit vague as to the exact locations, but we were sent to somewhere north of the town of Lanciano, Arrieti I believe, and I took up a position on the reverse slope of a hill overlooking a small river – the Germans, prior to our arrival, had occupied it. I was walking along a goat track by my company HQ when I trod on an antipersonnel mine (jumping-jack) – the type that, when trodden on, jumps up in the air for about two metres then explodes sending out 300 or more metal pellets. I even survived all these, not one touched me, though my Havildar, walking behind me, was badly wounded and evacuated. My company cook in the cookhouse, thirty or so metres away was hit as well.

It was early spring time and we had some nice weather so I took off all my clothes and put them in the stream/river below me and left them there all day with a rock to hold them down. This treatment, at last, got rid of the lice that I had acquired during the Cassino battle. I was now given my biggest command of the war, a force called 'DOG' Force. This had to guard the left flank of the Division. I had my own company, one other from the bn., and one from the Ghurkhas plus a squadron of tanks and could call on the Division artillery for support, when, and if necessary. I went round and reorganised the defensive positions to my liking. As a matter of interest I took over from another major called Mitford of the Ulster Rifles regiment. He was the brother of the famous (infamous?) Mitford sisters – one of whom was the wife of the fascist Oswald Mosely, and the other one who was a good friend of Adolf Hitler, no less. The Major himself had been part educated in Germany and, no doubt, some of the youth brainwashing there had sunk into him. I spent the night with him before taking over and we spoke about many things including how he had gone on patrol behind the enemy lines and met and spoken to Germans. He was not at all anti-German and even spoke well of the regime and Goebbels in particular. I got the impression that he was a very good soldier, with a regular commission. He was killed later in Northern Italy. Thankfully, I did not have any trouble while in command of this force.

Halfway between our and the German lines there was a farm known as Yanks Farm, presumably because the owner could speak a little American/English. I decided one night that I would go and visit this farm. On the night I set off with three men – the farm was about 500 metres in front of my forward posts. When we got to the gate and pathway leading to the house I, as usual, dropped off my men and crept up towards the front door listening very hard. I listened even harder at the front door itself and did hear low murmuring within. I took a chance and knocked, very gently not knowing what to expect – for all I knew the Germans might have been inside! The door was opened and when I announced that I was English the farmer, in a sort of English, invited me in to meet his wife and child. I did not stay long particularly after he told me that a German patrol had been there that very night and left about an hour before I arrived. He obviously did not approve of the Tredescis (Germans).

A little later the Germans must have decided to withdraw as I recall being given the job of advancing towards villages and small townships. This sounds easier than it really was, for one didn't know for sure if the Germans had pulled out or not and the only way of finding out was to walk in and hope for the best. I remember one particular township called Chieti, quite a big one, anyway bigger than a village. It was set up on top of a hill surrounded by its farming fields. I marched in very warily. There did not seem to be anybody about, very odd I thought (remember they had been our enemies until a couple months or so ago). I arrived in the town centre and stood waiting for something to happen. Eventually one man came out and shook hands. He turned out to be a doctor. Then many more emerged from the houses and a lot of cheering took place. From their point of view, of course, it was also pretty tricky for they did not know whether the Germans would come back and they did not know anything about us – and they had certainly not seen Indian troops before – and how friendly would we (their recent enemies) be? As it turned out we all got on well and much wine was brought out. I had drinks with the mayor and was asked to take messages from him and his family to other members of his family in Naples, as they had not heard anything from them for months. A couple of months later I happened to visit Naples and was treated royally on delivering the messages. They had two delightful daughters – I wish I could have stayed longer but alas, I had to return to my bn. for, as I said earlier, the bn. had left the Division for good. The Division went on to continue its thrust up Italy against the Gothic Line and the Axis (now mostly Germans) had been driven out of Italy.

After Cassino fell, Rome followed suit. I was given permission to take a party of our men to Rome and I recall camping for the night under the old Roman overhead aqueduct to the south of Rome – on Route 66. My party consisted of about 50 men i.e. Muslims, Sikhs, Dogras and myself, the only Christian. The next day we drove into the town and went to the Vatican to visit St Peter's. We were walking/clomping around in our boots and came to a brightly lit edifice; when the men asked me what it was – I was stumped and was about to give some sort of explanation when a quiet voice behind us announced that it was St Peter's tomb! Looking round I saw our informant was an Indian priest who, it turned out, was attached to the Vatican. We then continued our tour under his expert guidance. At the end he asked me whether I, and my men, a mixed bunch of religions if ever there was one, would like to meet the Pope himself. I of course said we would and he shepherded us into a large reception room in which there were about 150 or so seats. We sat down and waited. When most of the seats had been taken the Pope (Pius X11) entered and welcomed us with the little English that he could speak, after which he got up and walked out and away. This Pope was severely criticized after the war for not speaking out against the horrors being perpetrated by Hitler and his regime. (I think that I have read somewhere that he eventually died of hiccoughs!)

When we got up to go we were directed to a door at the back at which a man was seated by a table. My men, thinking that they were going to be asked to pay something for this privileged visit, were reluctant to go though this door so I took the plunge and went ahead to find that the man at the table was issuing us all with a little envelope which contained a small medal and picture of the Pope – free! I still have this medal as I write.

Chapter 20 : 1944

Italy, Brindisi, Palestine

Meanwhile our bn. was sent down to Toranto to await shipping to take us out of the war and to Haifa in Palestine. While waiting I was sent over to Brindisi (with two companies) to garrison the port and was made OC Troops, a command I did not take too seriously and we had many riotous parties. A bunch of us (including the CO who came over from Toranto) went for a two-day party to Bari. When I got back to Brindisi the young officer I had left in charge told me that the local Italian dignitaries had been complaining of all the rowdiness, particularly at night time. I couldn't stand for this so I arranged for them to come and see me in my office.

Before they arrived I lined up about twenty of my men, including tall, bearded, and turbaned Sikhs all with bayonets fixed and they formed a passageway through which these dignitaries would have to pass. When they had passed through this ominous avenue, and the sentries at my office door – I indicated for them to stand in front of my desk – by this time they were in no mood to complain. I asked them what they wanted to see me about, and they answered me in unison, saying how pleased they were to have us around and would I go along and have drinks with them. Ah! Well, all's well that ends well.

In due course, and after many other parties here and there, we embarked for Haifa and Palestine, reaching there in about July or August. The bn. was given a site on top of Mount Carmel, but I was sent off with my company to guard the CRL (Consolidated Refineries Ltd), this was located on the outskirts of Haifa. I/we used to go to the many bars and cabarets in Haifa where I got to know a lot of the barmen and artiste/s. One barman (Raul) and his partner (Rachel) used to take me to places of interest around the area – one was the original kibbutz where Raul was a part-time kibbutz policeman. On another occasion a club owner got completely drunk (his

Russian girl friend had gone off him) so I collected all the money, and there was lots of it, from the till, put it in a sack and took it all back to my camp. None of his friends and guests present seemed to think anything of this. The next night I took the sack back to him and he too didn't give it much thought – didn't even bother to count it! A little later I rejoined the bn. on the top of Mount Carmel where we were in tented accommodation. I have not mentioned this before but on taking over the Sikhs I did what all my predecessors had done before me, which was to keep the Sikhs fully occupied and busy. For any infringement of discipline the punishments that were handed out were twice or three times as severe as those handed out to the other castes (PMs and Dogras). I had an arrangement with my Sikh orderly that if he knew of any drinking that was taking place in any of the tents at night time then I was to be informed. I would go and get a bottle of whisky from the mess and, as if by chance, would arrive in the tent where I would join them until I deemed them to be past the stage of causing any trouble which was early morning. I would then depart and at 6.30a.m. when we had the morning PT sessions, I would get these men into a separate squad and make them do handstands, cartwheels, somersaults and other equally headsplitting exercises! I would add that I did the same as they. A comparatively new officer, though about the same age as myself, was attached to my company. He said that he thought that I was unnecessarily rough with my men but I told him that the Sikhs had to be kept well under control otherwise they were liable to ferment trouble. Personally I was very proud indeed to be the Sikh company commander, had complete confidence in them and had many happy times in their company. In passing I would mention that after I left the bn. to go back to India this same officer was given command in my place and he put into practice his ideas of easy discipline. Within the month there was a near mutiny with the men and he was, I believe, relieved of this command. There is one other incident that I was involved in and which is quite relevant in these days of drug addiction. One morning I was going round my company lines and in one tent I noticed three men still lying on their beds (charpoys). As they should have been on parade I put them under arrest and sent them, under an escort to the Guardroom to await the CO's disciplinary 'orders'.

With the Maharajah of Patiala (senior Sikh Prince) on his visit to the Bn. in 1944. The Bn. had just returned from the Italian campaign and was stationed on Mount Carmel, Haifa.

At 12 noon I had the men marched in and I read out the charge. The CO, who had many more years of Indian Army experience than I, had the men marched out again and then rounded on me saying that the men were authentic drug addicts who received their weekly ration of drugs from the regimental Medical officer (MO) but that, as the supply had been delayed and the men had not get their allotment, they were entitled to stay off duty until they did get it! In fact, I went nosing around after this incident and found that quite a few men, some NCOs, were on drugs but they were all perfectly good soldiers provided they got their drug ration.

I never felt I was in any kind of danger wandering about Haifa – always in uniform. I would have been much unhappier if I had been a British Palestinian police officer – they were detested. While there, I was made president of a Court Martial that had caused quite a stir. An Indian soldier, of a very low caste, had written scurrilous letters to the press and senior officers and I had to try him. I was given two junior officers on my court but they had never been anywhere near a Court Martial in their lives, nor for that matter had either the defending or prosecuting officers! I myself was no military law expert. I had attended three Court Martials but merely as an observer and once as the most junior officer in a court of five. I pointed this out to the Army Legal Authority (in Jerusalem) but was told to get on with it and use my common sense. In the end I found him guilty, sentenced him to 6 months' imprisonment and dismissed the service. The proceedings must have passed muster as the sentence was promulgated and I heard no more on the matter.

At this period of time there was much unrest in the country – mostly anti-British with the Jews clamouring for independence. They had their secret societies whose object was to disrupt the British administration as much as possible. They did this by blowing up various places e.g. St David's Hotel, in Jerusalem, police stations etc. etc. They did not try to do anything to the CRL, thank God.

Later, I was posted with my company to Jerusalem. While there I formed a Guard of Honour for Emir Abdullah of Jordan while he was visiting the British governor. Abdullah had been a friend to Lawrence of Arabia who had elevated him to the rank of Emir after the First World War. Soon afterwards we 'made' him a King. We (not the Emir and I!) had some riotous times in Jerusalem and I got in to a bit of trouble with the military police – nothing serious. Then one day, I was told that I had been recommended to attend the Staff College, Quetta (nowadays in Pakistan). I had twice previously been recommended but on both occasions had been turned down as I was under the minimum age required i.e. 25. Two other officers in Palestine were also due to attend – and we would be sailing from Suez in about two weeks' time. I managed to wangle a jeep to take me there – the other two decided to go separately – keeping well away from me! So I was on my own. Unfortunately I left Jerusalem with one or two bad marks to my name with the military police, however I was out of their reach. When I got to Suez I got into bad company – with the port detachment officer of the South African division – a major. He was the most wrinkled faced man I have ever known, being about 60+ of age.

I never saw him eat anything and he seemed to survive on South African brandy; barrels of which he was required to send on to his division. He tried to get me to join his regime, which I did for a few days! I ran into one or two spots of bother on account of him. When I was asked my name and address I always gave the regiment's address in Jerusalem knowing that by the time the bad news arrived there I would be on the high seas heading for India. How right I was.

Back in Jerusalem the CO had got himself in to deep trouble – so much so that he was relieved of his command. Another officer, with no war service, took command and all my chickens came home to roost to this new CO. I got to know about this by the other officers writing and telling me! Incidentally their letters to me were intercepted by the censors and then passed onto this CO. There is a sequel to all this which will come out later in my narrative.

Chapter 21 : 1944

Leaving MEF, Return to India

I embarked for India from Suez at the end of December 1944. I was, as I said earlier, going to attend the Staff College, at Quetta – which is right up on the Western edge of the sub-continent in the mountainous region of Baluchistan bordering on Afghanistan. It was quite a large military station having the Staff College there and two infantry bns. including a British parachute bn. After about 10 days I went down with a bad bout of bronchitis and this was followed by an attack of dysentery. I was in hospital for about 5 weeks and was then told that I had missed too much of the course and so lost my place which was most unfortunate for, without the staff college behind one, further promotion beyond the rank that I held as Major would be jeopardised. Anyway there it was. When I was discharged from hospital and, not having anything to do or anywhere to go to, I decided I would take some leave (I had not had any for 4 years) and go and see my parents in Ranchi (Bihar). On the way I went via Delhi where my elder sister had risen to the rank of Commodore of the Women's Royal Indian Naval Service (WRINS).

In Delhi I had some tooth trouble so arranged a visit to an Army dentist. His surgery turned out to be a disused garage with no electricity and poor lighting – I remember it all too well. A wheel, which he motivated by pumping up and down with his left leg/foot, drove his drill and all this while he tried to drill a hole for a filling. I was fearful that his hand would slip and the drill go through my cheek!

While I was in Delhi, and not a little down in the dumps, I thought that I might try my hand at a bit of clandestine soldiering. So I went to see the Director of Military Intelligence at GHQ (he was a 16th Punjab officer) and he thought I was mad but gave me a letter to a colonel in charge of some secret organization (whose name I forget) in Calcutta. When I got to

Calcutta I inquired as to the whereabouts of this office I was looking for and was told it was in a terraced house on the outskirts of Calcutta. There, in one of the two rooms were two WAC (I) girls. I chatted to them for a while then was called in to see the colonel. He told me that he was organizing the dropping of small groups (one officer, two interpreters and two signallers) behind the Japanese lines into French Indo-China (now known as Cambodia and Vietnam), with a view to contacting dissidents and, if possible, our POWs. It all sounded a bit hazardous but before making up my mind I asked if I could talk to someone who had actually operated on any of these incursions. He said that, unfortunately, no one had, as yet, returned from any of them! I said that I would get in touch him at the end of my leave. In the meanwhile he told me I had to keep the whole business secret and not mention it to anyone.

My parents had come to Calcutta to meet me and it was also where my youngest sister was stationed; she was serving in the Women's Auxiliary Corps (India) WAC (I). She was living in a hostel for these girls. That evening I went to pick up my sister at her hostel and found her talking to one of the two girls I had met earlier on. She recognized me, and my sister, knowing the girl and where she worked, put two and two together and guessed what I was up to – so much for security!

From Calcutta I went up to Ranchi to stay with my parents (he was Chairman of the Joint Public Services Commission for Eastern India). I had been told, when I left hospital in Quetta, that after 6 weeks I must get myself passed as medically fit so I got admitted to the hospital in Ranchi in order to undergo various tests. That very night I started to feel ill and by the next morning I was diagnosed as having acute bronchitis, which, in a few days, developed into chronic pleurisy. Before this pleurisy righted itself (I understood later, that I was very lucky to have lived through it) I had a recurrence of dysentery, bacillary this time. The usual treatment for dysenteries in those days was the dreaded enema but as this did not seem to work with me I was subjected to a new cure – *penicillin.* This treatment then consisted of having to lie on one's face, while an orderly, or nurse threw, dartlike and vertically, a hypodermic needle into the buttocks. The needle was then affixed to the hypodermic and a sizeable quantity of fluid injected. This caused bruising and so alternate buttocks took their turn. Furthermore this ritual had to take place, without fail every three hours, night and day. If one should miss a treatment then the whole procedure had to start again. As I was on a three-day treatment regime I got very sore indeed by the end. At the end of all this I was sent off on sick leave to recover. I went up to Darjeeling and while there the Japanese surrender took place so I was saved from that rather hazardous operation into Indo-China.

When my leave was up I had to report to my bn., which had returned to India after the war in Europe ended. The bn. was now in Sialkot and the CO was the man who had taken over in Jerusalem and where my escapades had been brought to his notice. On my arrival he had the 2nd in command march me in to his office where he said that he would be watching my activities very closely and hoped that there would not be any trouble. I carried on with my duties but decided that I would be better off elsewhere and asked him to recommend my return to the Staff College again. He refused saying that he personally did not know me well enough and that if I wanted to go there I would have to apply and recommend myself – so I did just that!

By this time the Director of Military Training in India (Delhi), a Major-General, happened to be the Brigadier for whom I did an operation in the Matmata Hills of Tunisia. Although the list had been closed he organised my re-acceptance. I stayed with my bn., (now stationed in Peshawar) until departing for the Staff College, Quetta. Before doing so, I had made myself very useful to this doubting CO – so much so that he said that he was going to have me posted back again after my course as his second-in-command! The short stay I had while the bn. was in Peshawar was quite interesting. The town is one of the old North-West frontier towns and when I was there it still had its perimeter wire and other defensive works around it to protect it from marauding Pathan incursions from the hills about thirty miles away where the famous Khyber Pass led into Afghanistan. The Army had contingency plans for any sudden attack and we had to be prepared for all eventualities. The British had been paying the hill tribesmen for many years just to keep them peaceful but quite often the tribesmen would break this arrangement and then frontier wars would begin. I recall that six of us young (and fit) officers were sharing the usual chummery but, in order that we would not be molested or have our belongings stolen during the night, we hired a 'chaukidar' to mind us. He was a very old man who had to be carried to our quarters by his grandsons and deposited on a 'charpoy' (bed) on the veranda each evening and there he slept the night through. This was really protection money as he was quite useless as a guard but if we hadn't paid for him, no doubt his relatives would have invaded our privacy in one way or another.

When I was up at the Quetta Staff College (also on the border of Afghanistan country) we would go up into the hills to do various exercises and there much the same sort of thing was happening. We would see the local tribesmen sitting on the hills 'guarding' us from attack by their brothers – for this they also got paid protection money and everyone was happy. In our bn. we had quite a number of Pathans and even one officer – a Mahsud. They all, even the officer, would go on anti-British raids while on leave, but when back and serving with the regiment they were loyal and excellent soldiers.

Chapter 22 : 1946

India, The Staff College and After

The Staff College course was of 6 months' duration. I did not exert myself unduly but kept pretty fit playing quite a lot of rugby and enjoying the social life. At the end the Commandant, at my interview, told me that I had passed, just, and that I was posted to a staff appointment in Southern Command, Madras. I demurred saying that I wanted to go back to regimental duties rather than, what I considered, boring staff duties. He said that I had not been trained as a Staff Officer in order to go back to regimental duties. I arrived in Madras as GSO (2) in the HQ there. As soon as I arrived I went in to see the Brigade commander and asked him to arrange for me to go back to my regiment. His reply was much the same as that of the Staff College Commandant. While in this HQ I had got to know a WAC (I) (Women's Auxiliary Corp (India)) Junior Commander who was on the staff as a Staff Captain. Within four months I was engaged to Greta Priestly and married on 20 November 1946, in the Connemara Hotel, Madras. We went up to Ootacamond for our honeymoon and stayed in a Maharajah's palace, actually, in a two-roomed bungalow set into the side of the mountain with a secret tunnel leading up to the main building. The bungalow was used to house his girlfriend(s).

While in Madras I came to know that my original bn. of the 16th PR – the 3rd bn., was now a parachute regiment. In passing I would mention that the Indian Army had a completely different way of raising parachutists. In the British army, volunteers were asked for and men were selected from those volunteers. This 3rd bn. was an ordinary infantry bn. One day an order came from GHQ, Delhi that the bn. was now a parachute bn. and any soldier who did not want to be a parachutist could opt out. It is a matter of record that not one single man took this option. I wrote off to the CO of this bn. and asked him to have me posted back, which he accordingly did and in January 1947 I arrived in Malir, some fifteen kilometres or so outside Karachi. As the 2nd in command had been posted elsewhere I was appointed in his place. I was 27 years of age.

Not long after my arrival I was sent off to attend a parachute course at a place called Chaklala near Islamabad and which is now the capital of Pakistan.

I went to Chaklala with the some twenty newly joined recruits to the bn. to carry out the required 10 days' basic training programme. The first four days consisted of various exercises designed to strengthen the stomach muscles in preparation for the necessary landing and rolling on to one's side when hitting the ground. Although I considered myself pretty fit even before I went on this course it turned out to be a painful experience.

The planes we jumped out of were old American Dakotas, which carried 16 to 18 parachutists. Our parachutes were attached to a long 'static' line running the internal length of the plane. The fastening was a strap to the outside of the parachute envelope, which, when tugged, let out the parachute. This strap was affixed to this static line by a clip resembling that on a dog lead. We jumped out of a side door when a green light appeared.

The last thing one did was to check that the clip of the man in front of you was in position on the static line, and then it was your turn to jump. Being an officer I was detailed to jump first. On my first jump the instructor, who would stand at the doorway and guide us all out, was bit of a joker and just as I stood at the doorway and was stepping out he showed me a loose unattached clip and asked, "Is this yours sir?" but then I was already on my way out!

The plane would start its run at about 400 metres from the ground and descend to, say 300 metres thereby insuring that the tail was slightly up and unlikely to snag our opening parachutes. The descent would take about 40 seconds I recall. In those days we did not have reserve parachutes – so if yours did not open, that was your bad luck. On my fourth jump I had a 'high twist' but one does not know that the parachute is not opening immediately so you are free falling at great speed. As soon as I realized that my parachute was tangled I tried to untangle the cords as fast as possible because the land was getting closer and closer at an alarming rate. Finally I succeeded but only just and, of course, I had descended so far that when I did hit the ground I did with a resounding thump. Normally one lands as if one had jumped off a 4-metre high wall. I never took part in any free-falling jumping because, as far as the army is concerned, it wants you, and the rest of your 'stick' of jumpers to all land close together for operational purposes. I make no bones about it; I did not particularly like jumping as, no matter what, the ground in Pakistan is very hard and bruises, great and small were the order of the day. On the course previous to mine a Ghurkha soldier had landed on a farm plough and was cut into two pieces. Also attending the course was the CO of the Frontier Force Rifles. On his fifth jump he hurt his back but nevertheless carried on to the end after which it turned out that he had hurt his vertebrae in three places – but he couldn't opt out in front of his men so carried on regardless. It must have been agonising for him to continue. I recall that on one occasion there was a very strong wind blowing and our planes went round in circles over the dropping zone. The pilots were trying to decide whether to cancel the drop, which they did and turned for base – that is all except for one – our pilot carried on, thought it would be OK and discharged us. On hitting the ground our parachutes being still open were caught by the wind, but before we could engineer their collapse, we were dragged and bounced unceremoniously over the hard landing area, sustaining even more bruises in the process!

When I got back to my bn., for economical reasons, the amount of jumping practice was restricted so every now and again, when exercises were carried out, the number of men who actually jumped was limited. My CO liked jumping and consequently thought I must like it too. How wrong he was, nevertheless when it came to allocating who was to be chosen to jump he always said that he had wangled it so I would be the lucky one! After a few months in Karachi the bn. was posted up to Quetta. In August 1947 India and Pakistan were granted independence.

Chapter 23 : 1947

India, Pakistan, Partition, Independence

While we were in Quetta, India and Pakistan gained their independence on 27 August 1947 under the then Viceroy of India, Earl Mountbatten of Burma. The Labour Party was in government in the UK at the time. On the night of the 26th the Indian and Pakistani officers in the station took over the club for the festivities. Greta and I were invited by an Indian Army doctor to attend. I believe that we were the only English people at this historic event. Before midnight the senior officers present each gave a speech and I'm glad to report that not a single word of criticism was uttered all night long against the British – on the contrary they praised the British for their fairness and the military traditions that were handed down and many of which are maintained to this day. I believe that the Army Regulations are almost the same now as they were in the days of the 'Raj' – even using the English language!

It has always been my view, a view that was held by many Indians and Pakistanis, that the transfer of power at such short notice was grossly unfair to both sides. It should have been carried out over about five years giving time for junior officers (of the army and administration) to learn their bigger responsibilities, and facilitate the transfer of power in a more orderly fashion.

The next morning, after the declaration of Independence, reality set in. That trouble would follow the division of the sub-continent had been foreseen. Let me explain:

> During British rule there had been comparatively little inter-communal rioting – some certainly – but it was contained in the last 60 or 80 years. I refer now particularly to the Punjab (the land of five rivers). It had become a very productive and fertile region due

to all the canals and water distribution – not to mention the roads and railways. As a result it was very densely populated. The population had become very mixed as well, with Hindu, Sikh and Muslim villages co-existing comparatively peacefully alongside each other.

When partition came, a line was drawn roughly from the Himalayan foothills through the centre of the Punjab along the Ravi River and thence south to the Indian Ocean. This meant that on the one side e.g. India there were many many villages made up of Muslims – a minority in a predominantly Hindu/Sikh environment. While on the other side, now Pakistan, the reverse was the position. The demarcation line between these two regions needed to be patrolled and guarded. It was the job of the Punjab Boundary Force (PBF) to do this – much easier said than done. Once one atrocity had been committed on one side, in no time at all, a retaliatory and similar one was committed on the other and this escalated into the most horrendous massacre the world has ever seen. It is said that over a million died the most terrible deaths during this holocaust. Even to this day I lie awake at nights reliving the awful sights I was unfortunate enough to witness.

A day or two after the partition the bn. left Quetta to join the PBF. Our colonel was promoted to brigadier and I then assumed command of the parachute bn. at the ripe old age of 27. It was to be a harrowing experience. The bn. was posted to Gurdaspur town on the south bank of the River Ravi. This was to be my responsibility. I was, incidentally, the only British officer in the bn., the others being either Sikhs, Muslims or Dogras – all excellent men.

My area to be covered was about 15 miles one way and 15 the other along the riverbank and a further 15 miles south. In the area there were many, many villages both Sikh and Muslim. I would state now – there was no law in the land. The magistrate was not to be seen, the Superintendent of police was keeping a very low profile so that left me responsible for law and order. There were massacres being committed all round me – too horrible to relate. One of my jobs was to collect the Muslim refugees into safe staging sites, sometimes 6–8000 of them and then escort them to the Ravi bridge and see them safely across the bridge into Pakistan. No easy task as the Sikhs would lie in wait in the long maize crops and make raids into the slow moving columns of the sick, elderly, children and stragglers. They would hack their way into these unfortunates with their long 'kirpans', a traditional Sikh sword about one metre long. One must remember that the Muslims were committing the same sort of brutality on the fleeing Sikhs on other side of the Ravi River.

I would go round to the Sikh villages and speak to them and ask them to desist from their actions. I always went with just a driver of my little jeep. I would never be armed with anything but my flywhisk and I felt perfectly safe. I went into one village that I had heard was responsible for atrocities and towed a trailer behind. When I got into the village I called for all the 'elders' and told them what I had heard and ordered them to tell their people to put all their weapons into the trailer. This they did, with some grumbling, and I then drove off to the nearest river and tipped them all into the river. The fact that I felt safe was entirely due to years and years of my predecessor's fair and incorrupt administration and hence the habit of obeying was ingrained into the people. On another occasion I was passing though a fairly deserted (Muslim) village and saw some Sikhs looting it. I got out of my jeep with my flywhisk, and entered the house where there were five or six of them, all armed with their kirpans and first I laid about me with my flywhisk then started kicking them on their shins with my boots whereupon they fled through the doorway and windows. Not one of them threatened me at all in any way.

On yet another occasion I was passing through a village and saw some looters behind a house. I got out and told them to get into my jeep; there were four of them. When I got back to a site where I was collecting refugees I asked around whether there was anyone there from the village from which I had just come. There were, so I selected two of them. I then had the four men tied to palm trees, cut a bamboo cane and told the villagers to administer a beating to the miscreants. I laid down that they must not hit above the buttocks level and that if they did then they would get similar treatment. As I recall it I restricted the number of strokes to 15 per man. This all took place in front of the refugees. When it was all over, the four men asked me to take them well away from the refugee staging area – so I piled them back in to my jeep and took them out of harm's way; on the journey we chatted about various things and when I let them go they were profusely thankful and didn't seem to bear me any grudge. The police superintendent came to my office some time later and said that he had heard of what I had done. I pointed out that I did that because I knew he would not have taken any action. He shrugged his shoulders and went on his way. In retrospect I don't think I did anything I had not experienced myself as a boy at school!

The next town to Gurdaspur was another called Batiala where a Frontier Force bn. was doing much the same sort of thing as I was trying to do. The colonel there, a British officer like me (the same one who hurt his back on the parachute training course) got so exasperated at the indifference shown by the town's magistrate that he arrested him and put him in the gaol. Unfortunately Nehru, Prime Minister of newly founded India, decided to come visiting and asked to speak his magistrate! On being told that he was in gaol Nehru blew his top and the officer was whisked across the border into Pakistan and flown back to the UK before worse should befall him!

The time came when my bn., which was 50% Muslim and 50% Hindu, had to split up with the Mussulmans crossing the Ravi bridge and entering their Pakistan. It was a very sad occasion. The Hindus were sorry to see their past colleagues depart and lined up on either side of the road leading to the Ravi Bridge to give us a good send-off. That was the end of the 16th Punjab Regt. I then took the Muslim sepoys back with me to Quetta where the reorganisation was to take place. When I got back I found Greta had moved out of our house and moved in with some other people. We then moved up to Lahore; I don't know why now. While in Lahore I went to the Army HQ there and met an officer who had been at Sandhurst with me. He was in the department dealing with the medals and awards so I asked him to let me have an MC medal, which I had never been given before – only the medal ribbon.

He said that he would speak to the general first and the next thing I knew was that my bn. from the Middle East days, the 4/16th Punjab stationed in Ferozepore were told to stage a parade for this ceremony. On the appointed day the general took my wife and me in his car all the way to the parade, some 100 kilometres away; en route he pointed out how different the countryside was from the days when he had first joined the Indian Army. I was waiting to be called forward to receive the medal from him when an old man in villager's clothes saluted and informed me that he was Subedar Daim Khan and that he had come from many miles away on hearing on 'the jungle telegraph' that this ceremony was taking place. You may recall that he was my Subedar when I first went 'into battle' in Eritrea in 1940. He had been taken prisoner at the retreat from Benghazi and spent the rest of the war in a German POW Camp. His presence there really made my day. It mattered more than the medal itself – the example he set lives with me to this day. A steadfast, unflappable, unassuming and really wonderful man.

Then came the time – (in mid December) 1947 when I secretly loaded up a lorry with all our possessions and one night crossed the border back into India from Pakistan. As trains from that country and that time did not connect up with Indian trains we went down to Bombay and from there I tried to get a ship going back to England. On arrival I was informed that this would not be easy as all the ships going that way were fully taken to transport the British regiments back for the men to be demobilised.

I registered with a shipping company for any ship leaving that port and going in a Westerly direction. After a couple of weeks we were offered a berth on a one-time pilgrim ship going to the port of Beira in Portuguese East Africa (now Mozambique). The journey was uneventful and we then moved up to Salisbury (Harare) in Southern Rhodesia (Zimbabwe) to look for a job. Before leaving the subject of India I would like to narrate an incident that took place many years later.

In 1987, exactly 40 years after the partition of India/Pakistan, my wife Margaret and I decided to go on a package holiday to India principally to visit Delhi, Agra, the Taj Mahal and Jaipur and with an extended stay on the Dall Lake in Srinagar (Kashmir). On arrival at Delhi airport we all went to our hotel that was sited on a small hill with a driveway leading up to the porched entrance, the drive then continuing on down the other side. We went in to dinner and halfway through the meal our courier came and informed us that a wedding procession was coming up to the hotel. We all piled out to watch. There was a quite a crowd already there lining the road and so we mingled with them – these watchers were three or four lines deep on either side. At the bottom of the drive the groom was waiting in a brightly lit carriage. In front of his carriage were two huge elephants with their mahouts on top.

Officers and Viceroy's Commissioned Officers of the 3rd (Parachute) Battalion of the 16th Punjab Regiment, 1947.
The author is seated fourth from right in the front row.

The procession started up the driveway with these two monsters leading the way on either side. When they got up to where we standing the mahout on the right hand side turned his head towards me and gave me a salute then, much to my, and everyone else's, astonishment, he directed his mount into the watchers, who had to give way, and brought the elephant up to me, made this huge beast kneel down and give me a salute with his trunk. I acknowledged this polite action by touching the offered trunk after which the mahout reversed his mount back on to the road to continue the procession. Now this mahout did not know me from a bar of soap – all he could have seen in the fading light was an elderly white-haired, white-moustached man who he must have surmised had been a member of the old Raj. This incident has been one of my most treasured and proud memories for, in my opinion, he was paying homage not to me but to the fair and incorrupt regime that had ruled his country in former years.

In passing I would like to relate a happening which bears out what I have just stated. My father retired as Inspector General of Police just after Independence was declared and applied for a very prestigious appointment in the new regime as Chairman of the Joint Public Service Commission for Bengal, Bihar, Orissa and the Central Provinces, an area five times the size of Britain. The duty of this Commission was the selection and appointment of applicants for senior posts in the administration. There were quite a few other applicants for the job, some judges, all of whom were indigenous to the country. When my father entered the room for the interview, to his chagrin, he recognised three of the board who, over a period, he had imprisoned for anti-British/establishment activities. Nevertheless he got the appointment which he held for the required number of years and, not only that, on his retirement, he was recommended for, and got, a knighthood. I can only assume that he not only fulfilled his role satisfactorily but was also known to be incorruptible.

Chapter 24 : 1948

In Africa, The Rhodesias (Zimbabwe and Zambia)

I have written elsewhere of the departure of my wife Greta and myself from India after the partition and formation of India and Pakistan and also the departure of British officers from the Police, Army and Civil Services. We left Bombay and headed for Beira, the port of Portuguese East Africa. From there we went to Salisbury (now called Harare) in Southern Rhodesia (Zimbabwe), and stayed in the Meikles Hotel. I bought myself a second-hand car but I was required to take a driving test – after having passed the test in India some nine years before, in 1939. I arrived for the test that was being taken by a grumpy-looking woman police officer. At the end of it she informed me that I had failed and would have to take it again in three weeks' time. Before that happened I went to a driving school to have refresher lessons. There, they told me that the policewoman had had a row with her boyfriend and everyone who took the test on that day had been failed! Anyway, three weeks later while re-taking the test and driving around Salisbury, I chanced to see Greta walking along and pointed her out as my wife whereupon the policewoman cheerily informed me that she had just got engaged. Surprise, surprise, I passed the test this time!

While in Salisbury, by chance I met up with a previous army colleague of mine whom I had known in Madras and so joined the company he was running called Pan African Roadways (a road haulage organization). Initially I was paid £5 per month, as it was known that I was being paid my Army pay for the next nine months. In due course I was made branch manager in a town called Umtali. I ran that office successfully for about eighteen months, but as the government had taken exception to the profits we were making by carrying the highest grade of goods, and leaving the state railway to move the lower-priced cargo, they handicapped the enterprise by various means. One morning I read in the papers that the company had ceased trading altogether which left me without a job.

While employed in Umtali I had purchased a small bungalow with a large unmade garden that I also proceeded to shape and cultivate during this period. I had started a correspondence course for a B. Comm. Degree and was enrolled as an external graduate of the University of Pretoria. In the meantime, our daughter (Felicity) was born in November 1948.

Chapter 25 : 1949

Move up to Lusaka, The Provincial Administration

I knew some ex-Indian Army friends who were working for the Northern Rhodesian (now called Zambian) government in Lusaka so I decided to go and visit them and see if I could get a job up there. I joined a large construction company (John Howards) in their accounts department, as I thought it might help me with my degree – but I stipulated that I would only try it out for three months, as I was not at all sure that accountancy would appeal to me. How right I was. After the three months I happily resigned. While in Lusaka I stayed in a bungalow with three other ex-patriots also working for John Howards. Greta and Felicity stayed in a hotel in Salisbury waiting to see what I would do.

Talking to my friends in the Lusaka Secretariat, they said that they had heard there might be a job going as a District Assistant in the Native Affairs Dept and suggested that I apply for it. They were not too hopeful, for by now the Colonial Office in London mostly filled these jobs. Anyway, it was worth a try, so I applied and here we come to another instance of the method of selecting officers for the administration of the Empire. After a few days I was asked to attend an interview with the second in command of the country's Native Affairs Department.

On arrival, I was shown into his office where he greeted me in a most friendly manner to put me quite at ease. He then asked me what I knew about cattle. This stumped me, as I knew absolutely nothing about farming – so I said I knew nothing about them. He then asked me: "If you saw an emaciated cow, and next to it another one which was obviously well fed, you could tell that one had been well looked after while the other one hadn't?" I agreed that I could. He nodded approval and then asked what I knew about cereals and crops generally. I again said I had never had any experience with them. He asked me a very similar question to the first one: "Could I tell the difference between maize stalks that were only a foot high and others that were 8 or 9 feet high?" I quickly asserted that I could; thereupon he got up, held out his hand and said that he thought that I would do well in the service! Shortly after, I received my posting to the Eastern Province, at Fort Jameson, as a District Assistant (Dec. 49).

Prior to the war, District officers were selected from Universities (Oxbridge mostly), and then sent out to the various colonies. They were known as the uniformed Officers. During the War this type of recruitment was suspended and so there was a shortage of District Officers to fill the gaps resulting from this temporary layoff. At the time that I applied for the post the colonies were allowed to recruit locally on the understanding that selected persons were not part of the Uniformed staff and that they would be employed, not by the Colonial Office (and therefore not pensionable), but by the Colony concerned, and that the tenure of office would be for ten years only. I was one of these District Assistants on a salary of £1000pa.

Chapter 26 : 1949

To Fort Jameson as District Assistant

Each Province is run by a Provincial Commissioner (PC) and under him there would be two or three District Commissioners (DC), each was allocated a district, which would be run from a district office called the 'boma'. Attached to a boma would be two to four District Officers or Assistants. When I got to Fort Jameson, (which also embraced the Provincial and District offices), much to my chagrin I was appointed PA to the Provincial Commissioner and not, as I had hoped, to the District as a District Officer. The Provincial Commissioner was away on tour when I got there, but he had left instructions that I could move into his very palatial house/bungalow until such time as he got back again. I then went to Salisbury and made arrangements for Greta and Felicity plus all our baggage and furniture to be moved up to join me. This was accomplished, but not easily, with the limited transport facilities available in those days. There was only one railway line starting from the north of Northern Rhodesia, running down south via Lusaka, Victoria Falls thence to Bulawayo and to South Africa. From Lusaka to Fort Jameson it was at least a 300 mile road journey over a rough corrugated hard surface. There was one government organised 'bungalow' en route for overnight stays but there were no shops or petrol stations.

When the Provincial Commissioner returned, I was allocated the old and original District Officer's house about 300 metres away from the boma. Although it was quite commodious, with a big wide flight of 12 steps leading up to the front door and four large rooms, plus a large reception area behind the front door, it had its disadvantages: there was no running water, no lavatory and no electricity – so we employed a boy called Sixpence (!), for whom we supplied a wheel barrow and two four-gallon petrol tins to go and get the water from a communal well situated about 300 metres away from our house. He would wheel the water back and, just behind the house, outside, there was a small walled off 'cubicle' with a 44-gallon drum suspended over the top. He would empty the water into this drum from which the water came down to a tap and an aluminium bath tub and wash basin. Also outside was the 'loo' shed with a seat and bucket. Every morning the prisoners from the local gaol would be marched around the officers' houses and dispose of the 'waste' buckets. There being no electricity we had to use paraffin lamps and also paraffin for the fridge. For the cooker we used firewood. Each morning a man would arrive on a bicycle with two four-gallon tins full of milk, on which he spread twigs and leaves to stop the milk slopping about on the rough journey. The house was so old that at night, when all was quiet, one could hear the woodworms munching their way through the woodwork in the window frames. We employed a houseboy to do our cooking, and a girl to help look after Felicity and her mother, and another boy to help in the garden.

Apart from the District officers, there were about 12 'messengers' on the strength. It was their job to help the District Officers in their work – but more about these later. As I say, I was attached to the Provincial Commissioner's office, which was not too bad really, and I got along very well with the PC, who was a retired Naval officer – by name Fox-Pitt-Rivers. But I did tell him that I wanted to get out into the countryside as soon as possible. I stayed with him for some eight or nine weeks until a replacement was sent up from Lusaka. This person was also a retired Naval officer and they should have got on well together, but they didn't. This chap tried to behave like a serving naval officer, saying, "Aye Aye Sir," using other similar naval jargon. So the PC would not let this man take over for some considerable time, until I eventually got him to agree to my being posted to the Fort Jameson District under the District Commissioner (Robin Foster – who later became Governor of Fiji). He immediately put me in charge of not one, but two Paramount Chiefs and their tribes, namely the Nkunda and the Ngoni. The former were alongside the East bank of the large Luwangwa River and in the tsetse belt with all the wild game roaming around; the latter tribe was situated upon the higher ground, where cattle (because there were no tsetse flies) could be grazed. The Ngoni comprised about twenty sub-chiefs each with about 15 – 20 villages while the Nkunda had 12 sub-chiefs with about 15 villages. They were also known as Native Authorities with 'councillors' supervising the various activities e.g. agriculture, housing, water, roads etc.

I would point out that this was in 1949 when I was 29/30 years of age; I could not speak the language and, of course, had no training in this sort of work. I soon decided I would go on my first 'tour' of my territory – and informed the DC I was going, whereupon he said he would come out with me to show me the ropes. I said that I would probably go for about eight or nine days. On the appointed day we set out with our retinue (I will give more details later of the procedures when touring). We walked most of the way and visited two or three villages en route, talked to the headman and discussed any problems that he, or the villagers under him, might have. As the sun started to go down we arrived at our camp for the night. Under the starlit sky, and by the light of hurricane lamps, we had our evening meal, opened up a bottle of whisky and chatted and drank. The next morning after breakfast he said; "Well, I think you've got the hang of it all right now, so I will leave you and get back to the boma. Good-bye!" That was my training for being a District Officer in charge of about 9,000 souls, their families, chattels and general well-being.

In the Province there would be attached the following other British officers: a senior policeman, an agricultural expert, a Water Dept person, a PWD man, a Forestry expert and a Class 1 magistrate who tried the more serious cases. The DC was a Class 2 magistrate and I was classified as a Class 4 magistrate with minimal powers i.e. sentencing up to seven days imprisonment. There were also a game warden and a ranger – a German left over from the last War!! I had had no legal training, but we were expected to take the Civil Service Law exam in due course, studying in our own time. I did this and found it very interesting.

The Eastern Province had Nyasaland on its eastern border, the Zambezi River to the South and Luwangwa River to the west. There were no industries but about sixty, mostly Afrikaans (of Dutch extraction), tobacco planters. Fort Jameson itself had one Indian shop from which we got our foodstuffs etc. If you wanted anything not available from the shop you had to write to one of the shops in Lusaka, or one of the towns on what was known as the line-of-rail, and they would send it to you. For my B.Comm. studies I had to write to the library in Bulawayo and borrow the textbooks from there – the whole procedure taking some weeks. I was allowed a fairly long time for the loan of books. The only means of communication was by road to the nearest railway station in Lusaka, some 300 miles away. There was an emergency landing strip for small aircraft but I don't recall it ever being used. Oh! And yes, there was a sort of 9-hole golf course. Social life, as in all the colonies, centred round the Club. Private parties were frequently organised but, of course, the people invited tended to be the same at every one of them, and conversation tended to be rather limited. We got used to it. We would wear evening dress, dinner jackets etc. at all evening functions. I had my car, which I had bought when I first arrived in S. Rhodesia. It was a big open top Ford V8 but as the roads barely existed, one did not use a car much.

Chapter 27 : 1950

A District Officer's Work Schedule

Normally a DO would go to the boma each day and there, if it was his turn, he would deal with the 'queue'. Every day people would come to the boma with their problems, queries, petitions etc. The queue never ended. It was more or less a permanent fixture of boma life. A clerk would be present and he would translate, (and advise), on each matter. One of the messengers would be at hand to give guidance in matters relating to tribal customs. These messengers were all from the tribal areas within the District/Province. They got their name from the days when they were the only means of communication – reputedly they carried the written messages attached to a cleft stick.

DOs were expected to spend quite lot of their time on tour of their tribal areas. I tried to get to them for about 8 – 10 days each month. There were no roads as such in my areas, so most of the touring was done on foot or, in my case, on a bicycle. There were no maps, but some rough sketches drawn up by previous DOs. I decided to try and overcome this handicap and make my own maps. I would take out a large notepaper pad, a compass, and a milometer fixed to the front wheel of my bicycle. As I cycled along the pathways I would make notes of any prominent landmarks, take the mileage, and compass bearings. Then when I got to my night stop I would draw up a map of the day's 'surveying', which would also include the location of the villages in relation to each other. On return to the boma, at the end of each tour, I would elaborate on this drawing. I obtained sheets of oilcloth, each about 18 inches square and drew on these with mapping ink – the 'maps' were based on my sketches taken on the tour. On completing this, I would get a piece of wood, like a runner's baton, pin one end of the oilskin map to the baton and roll it up for storage on a shelf. Then when I, or anyone else, went to that area they would pick up the roll and take it out with them. These were certainly not 'surveyologically' correct, but they were better than nothing. Finally, when I had covered my whole area I transferred all the information onto a large sheet of paper, about 5ft by 6 ft, and sent this off to the Surveying Dept office in Livingstone who congratulated me on my efforts. What's more, they produced a printout of the whole sheet and also small prints of the individual chiefs' tribal areas. No doubt this whole country has by now, been surveyed properly but I wonder what happened to this 'map' of mine!?

After completing a tour, the DO would have to submit a report on his travels which would then be read, not only by one's own Provincial and District Commissioner but it would go back to Lusaka to be read by the Secretary for Native Affairs – the head of the Native Affairs Dept. That way, he would have good knowledge of what was happening in the country but also, what DOs were up to. I personally used to give a tabulated outline of what I found and saw, such as the number of wells, dams, ploughs, cattle, crops and anything else I thought of interest – so by the time I finished a tribal area we could see at glance what was going on there – a sort of Doomsday Book.

Before I went off on a tour, 'ulendo', the following preparations had to be made. I would decide which tribal area I was going to, which chiefs I would be visiting, and which villages. Without any maps and no previous knowledge I could not do this without consulting the messenger who had been allocated to me – one Robert Msoro of the Msoro chief's area, an excellent man who was with me throughout my term of office. He could not speak any English so, for my first few tours, I took Michael (the office clerk) to act as interpreter. He had a great sense of humour and we got on well together (laughing our way round the countryside). In fact, I dropped him as soon as I could, as I reckoned I would learn the language much quicker if I did not have him to rely on. This decision proved right, for I passed my first exam in Chinyanga very soon. In fact, I also passed the final part within 14 months – I'm told this was a near record.

Robert Msoro would set out an itinerary for me, the villages etc. which I would visit and, most important, the order in which they would be visited; then he would arrange for messengers to go ahead warning everyone that I was on my way, to visit them.

Robert would also arrange for porters for all the baggage. A DO was entitled to take 18 porters for his personal baggage which would include a large tent, a tented bathroom, a small veranda, a bath tub and wash basin, camp bed and bedding plus, of course, food and drink. In addition, a further 4 porters were added to carry the baggage of the porters, messengers, and any other people who might join us, e.g. the chiefs and councillors. The day before we actually left, he would send a messenger ahead to the first few villages we were going to visit and another one further ahead to the village at which I was going to spend the night, so that the campsite would be ready on our arrival. For instance, when down in the Nkunda, where big game abounded, a zariba had to be constructed around my tent to keep the animals from wandering in to visit me. A large fire and a night's supply of firewood was also a prerequisite for a quiet night's rest. One could hear animals all around, including lions. I would sleep alone in my tented campsite, but the porters etc. would go and sleep in the village. I never felt afraid and, only in the Kaunda country, did I carry a gun – and that only in case I wanted to shoot game or birds.

Before arriving at a village the young boys would come out and meet me from some 300 yards away. When I got to the edge of the village all the women would be squatting down to greet me, meanwhile making the most unholy shrieking noise and at the same time slapping the insides of their thighs. They kept this up until I reached the centre of the village where the headman would be waiting to greet me and I would be invited to sit down on a very rickety chair or box. Only then would the women stop their noise and the talking begin. Actually, no one had much to say – though I would ask some questions to help me fill in my report. Then on we would go to the next village. Sometimes, if it was a fairly large village or near that of the chief, he would lay on a sing-song or whatever. These tended to go on all night, or until I got up to go to my campsite. In moderation they were quite pleasant, consisting mostly of the men getting into a circle and chanting as they went round and round. On arrival at a village, it was the practice of the headman to present me with a gift, which always consisted of a rather small chicken. In keeping with the British policy of never accepting presents, after I had left the village my messenger would give the headman a shilling. Sometimes I kept the chicken and had it taken back to the boma where I kept a chicken run for use in the future. But more often I ate it for dinner that night and then again cold the next day when I stopped for a lunch break. One would very very rarely come across a shop and then it would have an Indian owner whose trade was mainly in what was known as 'kaffir truck', that is to say, bolts of material, seed, tools, some foods and odds and ends. It is interesting to note that the shopkeepers had little say in what was contained in the bales of kaffir truck. They just ordered so many bales, which might include all sorts of things the wholesalers wanted to get rid of! For instance, they might enclose a 100 pairs of toenail scissors which the shopkeeper had no hope of selling. So he in turn, quite illegally, would make anyone wanting to buy something also have to buy a pair of toenail scissors whether they wanted them or not! Occasionally an African would decide he too would have a shop. He would come to the boma and get a licence – costing him one shilling. He would go off and buy a few bales and set up shop. Unfortunately they had no idea about restocking the shop and just spent the money as soon as they had sold anything and the shop would then close down. No amount of advice as to what should be done was heeded.

Sometimes we would get a request from medical practitioners asking us to help them in their research e.g. the incidence of leprosy and eye diseases. Most DOs ignored these requests but I really tried to help. In my areas I had a Leper colony (Seventh Day Adventists), and I used to visit them on my rounds and had very interesting discussions with them on all sorts of subjects. One medical researcher asked me to try to ascertain the incidence of leprosy in my area. I had to go to all villages and try and diagnose those people with leprosy. The villagers themselves would not let on if anyone in their village had leprosy, but I wasn't too worried about those. It was those who might have got it but did not know it. In order to find this out I had to look for telltale signs of the disease on the backs, chests and upper arms. The sign to look for was a light coloured patch about the size of a ten penny piece. On arrival at a village, for privacy's sake, I would collect all the men at one end of the village and all the women at the other end to carry out my inspection. They had to bare the upper parts of their bodies When I discovered a leprosy spot I merely made a note of the fact, ascertained the number of people in the village and worked out a percentage rate.

In fact in my 'parish' the rate turned out to be 1 in 100, which apparently warranted special attention. I believe a leprosy unit was eventually established in the area.

Another research I became embroiled in was the diagnosis and counting of people affected with eye problems, and I received written instructions on how to carry out this work – which involved the recognition of trachoma, conjunctivitis and two other eye problems. Here again, I lined up the villagers and made them look up towards me. I became quite good at diagnosis and carried on an interesting correspondence with the eye specialist who had come out from the UK.

The propagation of the Bible and Christian faith was quite a complicated affair in large parts of Africa and in my area it was no different. At some time or another, the various religions had divided up the area amongst themselves. My area housed Seventh Day Adventists, White Fathers (Roman Catholics), Dutch Reformed and the UMCA (Protestants). When they divided up the area they did not take into account the fact that the villagers were semi-nomadic; in as much as, when their crops failed to flourish they tended to move off to another unused site – so eventually the various missions were all mixed up. The local pastors would go round with bags of salt etc. and try to persuade any villages that had moved into their parish to convert to their faith – this of course caused some problems but we tended to let the missions sort themselves out and kept out the way! For my part, I was impartial and would go and stay at any one of the mission stations that were in my area. I enjoyed my stays with them all and found it very interesting to hear their views; one thing I went along with all of them on, was the promotion of education and the provision of schools. Where I could, I had schools erected and benches made for the children to sit on rather than squatting than on the floor. This 'accommodation' served me well later on, when I took my language oral exams these missionaries turned out to be my examiners and I noticed that I seemed to pass with just one mark over the pass mark!

My duties as a DO covered all sorts of aspects of administration. Everybody had to pay a set amount of tax each year and this had to be collected and accounted for. I was responsible for the budget of the two native authorities and, of course, for the keeping of the account books. I had an African 'treasurer' who did most of the work but I supervised him. Every month I would go to their headquarters and do a monthly audit. I noticed with one of them that the treasurer often seemed to have gone off by the time I arrived, leaving a note behind that he had taken the cash to Fort Jameson for banking. After this had happened two or three times I decided to make a quick dash back to meet him there and do a check on the monies – and found a discrepancy from the totals I had checked in books. He had disposed of quite a lot of money and so I had him arrested and charged. He was found guilty and sent to prison. When it was all over, the District Commissioner congratulated me but made an astute observation to the effect that I would now have to find another treasurer and then get to know what he would get up to as he would probably do much the same thing, only I would now have to discover his financial tricks whereas I knew how the last one had operated!

I mentioned that there were a few technical advisers at Provincial Headquarter in Fort Jameson and it was their job to think up the various ways of improving the lot of the tribes. They could not go and give direct orders to the Chiefs because the Chiefs would not pay any attention to them unless I, as their DO, personally issued the orders. I would summon an 'indaba' at the paramount Chief's village. There, the sub-chiefs, councillors and many headmen would attend. This would take place under the indaba tree. I would sit at a table with the expert adviser and In front would squat the Paramount Chief, behind him the sub chiefs and behind them again anyone else who might want to hear what was going on.

I will digress here to relate a story. My predecessor, with these two tribes, was a good DO but he was pretty rough with them. As a DO one had to get things done for their benefit – for instance build roadways, dams, schools, public buildings, cut fire breaks, and there wasn't always finance to carry out these tasks so we organized labour forces from the villagers to implement the plans. It was not really slave labour as it was for their own benefit. This was general practice and was observed everywhere. Anyway, the task forces were given the plans and time schedules for carrying out these works and the DOs would go, at regular intervals to see what progress was being made. Generally progress was slow, as no one was being paid.

So, to hurry them up one had two choices – the first one which I used to follow was to fine the local chief or supervisor and they did not like this at all. My predecessor always carried a long Boy Scout's pole with him wherever he went. When he got annoyed with anyone who prevaricated with him he would clonk them on the head with this pole. I once asked my messenger what the people thought of him and gathered that he was quite popular, in fact they preferred his 'justice' to mine for the next day, although they might have a lump on their skulls, at least their pockets had not been touched! On another occasion, I wanted to invest some of the tribe's surplus finances in shares or some interest bearing bonds, so I called an indaba. At this meeting I asked Robert to fetch me some small stones with which I intended to demonstrate how £1 (or stone) would accumulate interest and become many stones (pounds) if invested wisely. When Robert returned and placed the stones on the table, the whole meeting, chiefs included, got up and backed away a short distance.

I asked Robert what was going on and he said that the last Bwana always had a pile of stones on the table and threw these at any person present who caused trouble or asked any awkward questions! This DO left Fort Jameson for Kenya where he was promoted and made a District Commissioner – which post, I have no doubt, he fulfilled very well.

I was responsible for erecting buildings, dams across small rivers/streams, and roads. I would grab a piece of paper and draw what I thought was an adequate plan of what I wanted and then let them get on with it.

In those days DOs, who were in charge of areas that housed game, used to get up very early at dawn and do most of their touring on foot, during the cool of the day. They would stop and rest up until the evening when they would go off and shoot something for the pot or even game, large and small. I had a different regime. I would get up fairly late, have a leisurely breakfast then go off about my business, regardless of the temperature. I preferred to carry on touring/cycling in the heat of the day rather than try to rest/sleep in a very hot tent. As I was not particularly interested in shooting and fishing in the early evening, I would get back to my campsite and start work on my report, maps and then long into the night, by hurricane lamp, carry on my studies for the language exam, civil service law exam and also for the B. Comm. degree. When the time came for me to take the exams, the University would send the papers to one of the missionary stations and get them to invigilate over me. At first, I used to start off tours with a bottle of whisky, but I found that I used to drink nearly all of it on the first night, so gave up taking even that one, and thereby reduced my consumption very considerably.

On the subject of elephants, I would mention here that officers of the Provincial Administration (PCs, DCs and DOs) were permitted to shoot four elephants a year – this number was reduced to two shortly after I arrived. The tusks were sent off to an auction and the proceeds of the sales contributed towards the costs of educating their children at boarding schools in the UK. There were plenty of elephants in the area of one of my tribes i.e. the Nkunda. The trick was to shoot those elephants with big (profitable) tusks. To do this I got in touch with the game ranger who knew their whereabouts and he would direct me to where the larger animals were browsing. In fact, I shot my quota, but not without incident. I would add I consider myself lucky to be alive to tell the tale.

Having shot one, the news flashed around very quickly to nearby villagers who thronged around the corpse and cut off the meat for future consumption. They would cut off strips and then cook them over a fire, the strips being laid out on a grid of poles high up over the fire. The villagers were always only too willing to report any unruly elephants or hippopotamus and would ask to have them shot, that way there would be a plentiful supply of meat. I never acceded to their requests.

I found the work of a District Officer exceedingly absorbing and very fulfilling. One's life was entirely given over to the welfare of the tribes (sometimes referred to as Native Authorities) and I was even happier when I could converse in their language. We were certainly not overpaid and there was never any question of asking for, or getting paid for overtime. Wives of these administrative officers were left very much on their own due to the time their husbands spent on tours. For my part I used to tour for 7 to 12 days each month.

One day I returned from a tour and was told that the Chief Secretary had come to visit the boma at Fort Jameson. When I met him he told me that my name had been put forward to the Colonial Office in the UK to be taken on as a permanent District Officer in the Provincial Administration, but that the Colonial Office had turned down the recommendation on account of recently promulgated policy that no more DOs were going to be appointed (self government was not far off!). He went on to say that he could get me appointed as a Section Officer in the Secretariat – the governing body of Northern Rhodesia and that this appointment would be pensionable – this last led me to accept the appointment.

Chapter 28 : 1952

The Secretariat, Luaska, Return to the UK

My posting to the Secretariat arrived and I left Fort Jameson, with great regret, on 23 April 1951. At the top of this establishment was the Governor who at that time was one Rennie by name. He was responsible to the Colonial Office in London. Under him were the Chief Secretary, the Attorney General and the Assistant Chief Secretaries (ACS) who headed the various departments – each of the latter had two or three Section Officers of which I was to be one. I was posted to the Attorney General's dept – I was unfortunate, in that the ACS of this dept was an absolute stickler for details, a large number of which, to my mind, were of little importance. The practice there was that all letters would be typed in triplicate. One would go to the addressee, one would go into the relevant office file and the third into a file cover which would be passed round the offices – the theory being, I suppose, that everyone would know what was going on everywhere! (If one took the trouble to read everything that arrived on one's desk!).

There was a great shortage of secretaries, so one had to have an odd machine trundled into the office – this machine had a circular barrel on it and a mouth piece into which you spoke and which was translated into sound onto the barrel which was covered with some sort black stuff. When you had finished the machine was taken away to any other office that needed it and then at the end of the day the letters/messages were listened to (with earphones) by a stenographer who typed your letter (and all the others on this barrel) and delivered it back to you – eventually.

The first file I opened was one relating to the purchase of the remains of an Army Camp. I asked my secretary what had transpired in the past and she advised me to go down to the 'mortuary' and get the files being stored there. I duly went and to my astonishment found about ten files full of this subject. I read quite a few of them and got to understand that the man who had bought the contents of the camp at a government auction had supposed that this purchase included all the piping for water etc. leading to the camp. My above-mentioned ACS had managed to string this argument out for months. Anyway, I could not see that this presented much of a problem and, as the piping was not of any use to anyone else where it lay underground, I decided that this matter had gone on long enough so I wrote to the purchaser and told him to take the wretched piping and closed the subject – or so I thought – but I had not taken into consideration the progress of the third copy of my letter which was, of course, picked up by my ACS. He blew his top and said in words to the effect that there was plenty more life in the subject and made me cancel my decision and send out a letter of apology. I reckoned that without this sort of bureaucracy and prolonged unnecessary correspondence, he could hardly justify his position.

The Attorney General's responsibilities could be likened unto those of the Home Secretary in England and included on the one hand the maintenance of Law and Order i.e. the police and prisons and on the other, he administered the law through the courts and the solicitors. The courts may find a person guilty and then, wearing his 'Home Secretary's' hat he would go into the background of the crime to see if there were any extenuating circumstances before the sentence was agreed (promulgated).

One of my jobs was to carry out any orders etc. that the AG might find it necessary to issue wearing his latter hat. One of these was to make arrangements for the execution of men found guilty of murder, and then draw up the Death Warrants. The latter act involved me going to the Chief Secretary's office and asking his secretary to produce the black 'death seal' which she and I together then impressed on the Death Warrant with the seal press. She used to go absolutely white when I arrived at her door and I honestly think that she hated me – as if I had personally been involved. Once I had to go and get three seals for three executions to be carried out in one morning at half hour intervals. I thought she was going to faint when I told her this!

The work was not at all arduous and I found time hanging on my hands very often, so I decided that I would do a little research into the history and background of the death sentences that had been passed in the previous ten years or so within the colony. In all there had been something like 120 murders. In 82 of these, it was the wife who had been murdered. The rest were mainly 'friends' of the accused and nearly all the murders had been committed with a small hand axe (called, I think, a nkwanga), which all Africans in the bush used to carry as we would a walking stick. Very few, if any, of these killings had been premeditated but were done on the spur of the moment. It would seem that the perpetrator would be standing around with, as usual, the little axe in hand; if there was an argument it would be very easy, in a fit of temper, to lash out with this implement and the murder was committed. From this research I deduced that if this small hand axe were prohibited, there would have been hardly any murders at all! I had intended, when I had completed my research, to submit it to the Attorney General for his attention but I did not get that far as I left the service before I could do so.

On two occasions I had to carry out quite an interesting research. There were two men, unconnected but due to be executed – both for murdering their adulterous wives. In my researches I discovered that in the case of one of them, in his tribe it was quite common for the wife to have 'boyfriends' and adultery was not at all unusual – certainly not a killing matter and so this man was executed, while the other, where no such custom existed and adultery was considered a serious misdemeanour and therefore a reasonable excuse for murder, was merely found guilty of manslaughter and served a prison sentence instead.

I was involved in a case where the accused was found guilty, but there was doubt as to whether he was over or under 18 years of age. If over, he would hang, if under, then he would serve a prison sentence instead. There was no record of the date of his birth but he said that he was born in the year of the 'great rains'. In Africa, of course, there are heavy rains frequently, so I got in touch with the District Officer in this man's tribal area, and asked if there had been any known 'great, out of the ordinary, rains'. He was unable to give any firm answer but suggested that I get in touch with the District Officer who had been in charge at about the right time – the snag was that he had retired and was living in England. I was given his address and so wrote off to him. In due course I got a reply from this ex-District Officer who remembered one particular season when the rains were remarkably heavy and he gave me the year, so, with this information to hand, the man was given the benefit of the doubt and got a prison sentence instead of execution – such are the thin threads of life on which one's destiny depends.

The social life in Lusaka was much more varied than in Fort Jameson and the Club was larger with greater facilities, it even had an 18-hole golf course, which I frequented as often as I could. There was little or no grass on the fairways so the ball tended to go great distances! But it was better than no golf course at all. The greens were in fact ‘browns’, a circle of a mixture of sand and, I think, oil. They were very smooth with no undulations (borrows). I got my handicap down to 2. (For reasons that will become clear I did not play golf again for 25 years). It is of interest to note that while the British had to put up with this better than nothing golf course, soon after we handed over the colony and when independence was attained, money seemed to be forthcoming (from the IMF?) to build a first class course with completely grass fairways and greens all, of course, watered by a very expensive sprinkler system.

At about this time my domestic life was far from happy and I was not too content with my chairbound office job in the Secretariat. It then so happened that I received a letter from the War Office in England telling me that, on account of the increased activities of the Chnese communists in Malaya whose aim it was to take over the government of that country it had been decided to increase the size of the Malay Regiment from its one battalion to six bns. They were contacting ex-Indian Army officers as it was thought they would probably ‘fit in’ and offered a three year contract to re-enlist. The terms were not at all fair or, inviting, as no increased pension was included and, at the end of the three years, a lump sum of only £1000 would be granted. Furthermore no financial aid would be forthcoming to cover the cost of my return to the UK, and I would have to undergo a three-month retraining period with a British Regiment – the Gloucesters, because I had been out of the Army for three years – and I would have to drop one rank to that of a Captaincy. In spite of all this I decide to re-enlist. I had never done any jungle warfare – just the desert and Italy so this proved an added incentive.

Things were made even more unpleasant for when I informed the Northern Rhodesian Government that I wanted to go straight away, without giving three months notice, they demanded £500 from me (a lot of money in those days) –I can’t think why they did this now. On top of this I had, of course, to pay for my fare back to England and also for my wife and daughter. In spite of these many obstacles, I pressed on with my plans.

I made arrangements for my flight back to the UK and for a sea passage from Cape Town for Greta and Felicity who would follow, in due course, with all the furniture and luggage.

Having made this decision I had to wait for a few weeks and in the interim sent off to Malaya for some books on the Malayan language. When the plane journey was all booked, I was to leave from Livingstone airport on 24 May 1952. I left Lusaka by train (17/5/52), but before leaving, bought myself my first good camera. Up until then I had only possessed a very simple Brownie. This purchase nearly proved to be my undoing for when I arrived at Victoria Falls I went sightseeing around the Falls and very impressive they are too. They were in full flood with the water just crashing over the edge, particularly at the point known as the Devil's Gorge. About ten yards from the edge there is a statue of Livingstone (who 'discovered' the falls in his travels) and I decided to photograph myself (using my new camera with its self timing mechanism) standing next to him. I started walking backwards to get to a spot where I could set up the camera on it's tripod, then suddenly felt no more ground behind me and could only hear the roar of the falls, so I froze. It seemed like ages before I felt safe to take a step forward and onto firm ground. If I had gone over, no one would ever have known and I would have become a missing person. I am told, at this point, a fence has now been erected to prevent such an accident.

The return flight (to England) involved a stop over in Nigeria at Kano airport. I have been in some very hot places in my life and thought I would have got used to them, but I shall never forget the heat of that airport. We got out of the plane and went into the airport buildings and, while there, a large vehicle drove alongside our plane with a huge air conditioning hose which was thrust in to the passenger area to cool it down until we embarked again, but the heat was terrific – somewhere in region of 145 degrees (F). On arrival back in England it took me about a week to recover. I went and stayed in Oxford with my mother (at 97 Lonsdale Road in May '52) until Greta and Felicity arrived a few weeks later – in the interim period I went to London to get my orders and was informed that I had been posted to the Gloucester Regiment on 11 Sep '52 – the idea being that, as I had been out of the army for some years I would have to catch up on any new weapons/methods and would most likely be with them for a couple of months before going out to Malaya.

My time with the Gloucesters was fairly uneventful. This bn. had sustained huge casualties in a defensive position, where they were greatly outnumbered by Chinese forces in the war in North Korea in 1951. On being brought back to the UK it was stationed at Warminster carrying out duties as a demonstration unit for the Army Training school and also for the Joint Services Senior Officers Staff College, both of which were situated in that area.

I was put in charge of a platoon – quite a come down from my previous ranks! One day I was involved in an exercise and was going over my plan with the platoon when a young officer, also attached to this platoon, made what I considered a derogatory remark about my plan within the hearing of the men. I called him to one side, but within the hearing of the men, and told him that if he ever spoke to me again in that manner I would *not* take him up before the CO for insubordination – but would take him out into the countryside and there knock the bloody hell out him. I had no more trouble with him.

On another occasion I was out with this demonstration platoon for a defensive exercise for the Senior Officers' course – who all held the rank of colonel or brigadier. Before the lesson began I received a message that the normal course instructor was not able to attend and I was to take over in his place. I had done this exercise before and thought then that it was seriously flawed, however it was not for me to change it, so I carried on with the set course solution. I did notice that there was one brigadier present but who was standing to one side of the others. I did not recognise him. At the end of the exercise I, as usual, asked if there were any questions. Also present were two Polish colonels, and they put their hands up. They asked me what I personally thought of the defensive positions. This put me on the spot. I thought hard, and quickly decided that as I had nothing to lose I would come out with what I thought was wrong, i.e. the positions were all wrongly sited on the forward slopes of a hill – a position I and my company would have been in, had I carried out that attack while at Monte Cassino. The Poles were entirely in agreement with me and I think that the other officers went along with me too. A couple of days later I was told to report to the Commandant of the Staff College. He told me in no uncertain terms that I was wrong to criticise the course, however, he said he had read over the exercise and, as a punishment, told me to rewrite the exercise for the course curriculum – which I did – and it was accepted verbatim!

Chapter 29 : 1953

Malaya, Camp Commandant, Kuala Lipis

Finally I set off by air, from Heathrow on 29 December 1952; there was one stop at Karachi before reaching Singapore airport on 2nd January 1953.

First I went to Taiping, to the 2nd bn. The Malay Regiment and almost immediately was sent off on a language course in the Nee Soon barracks on Singapore Island. As I recounted earlier, I had sent off to Malaya for some Malay language books and so for months now I had been studying the books; but with no guidance as to pronunciation I could not get very far and so concentrated on acquiring an extensive dictionary of words and hopefully would get the pronunciation explained later. In fact, I must have learned some useful 1500 – 2000 words by the time I started the course. This dictionary came in very useful because I did not have to worry about learning it and could just concentrate on the grammar and pronunciation. Consequently I raced ahead of all the others on the course – in fact, after two weeks, the instructor, who was English, said that I was wasting my time there and I would be better off back with the battalion where I could my put knowledge into practice. So I went back to Taiping and there I was given the bad news that I would not be staying with the bn., but had been posted to Kuala Lipis to be Camp Commandant at the Brigade Headquarters there.

I did not like my posting as Camp Commandant of Brig. HQ because I had not rejoined the Army to be a Camp Commandant but to be a regimental officer. I told the Brigade Commander my views on this subject. He was very sympathetic, said he would try and transfer me but, in the meanwhile, I was to carry on as instructed. As it turned out this job was a sinecure for corruption as I soon found out. The local contractors, Indian and Chinese, were all over me and I was invited to meals etc. and was offered a car as well. To make sure that nothing like this could be pinned on me I obtained a loan (to buy a car) from Army sources where everything was official. I soon discovered all sorts of irregularities such as laundry, boot repair bills, food supplies and so on which I was required to sign as having been carried out (although they had not), before the contractors could be paid. My predecessor obviously had been doing very nicely as had one or two other officers on the staff. I reported this to the Brigade Commander, in writing, but he did not want to stir things up and just told me to clear the decks. However news of this letter of mine somehow got to the ears of the army SIB (Special Investigation Branch) in Kuala Lumpur, and later when I was on a jungle operation, a helicopter was sent in to bring me out and I was taken to Kuala Lumpur where I had to report the matter all over again to the SIB. In the event the Indian contractor, a JP by the way, was relieved of his appointment, two of the officers were brought back to Malaya (one from the Caribbean), and the Chinese food contractor lost his contract for food supplies – or so I was told. Some time later, when I was in another area, I decided I would to go and supervise the collection of my company's rations and lo and behold I recognized some of the men who had been employed by the Chinese contractor in Kuala Lipis. I had him removed from the contracting list.

While I was in Kuala Lipis I heard that accommodation for Greta and Felicity was available – but only in Kota Bharu, which is right up on the Northern coast where the Japanese invasion of Malaya started. There was no railway line to that town as the Japanese had dismantled the line for use on their infamous railway line to Burma during the war in the East and prior to their invasion of India. It was well known for its beautiful sandy beach and dipping palm trees, and was called *pantai chinta berha-i*, which loosely meant the beach of passionate love.

Some weeks later Greta and Felicity came by boat arriving in Penang, where I went to meet them and from there we went for a short holiday up to Fraser's Hill – a hill station in central Malaya. While we were there, back in the UK, Queen Elizabeth II had her coronation – in May 1952. Greta and Felicity then had to go to Singapore and get on a boat, a very small one I gathered, in order to get to their destination – Kota Bharu.

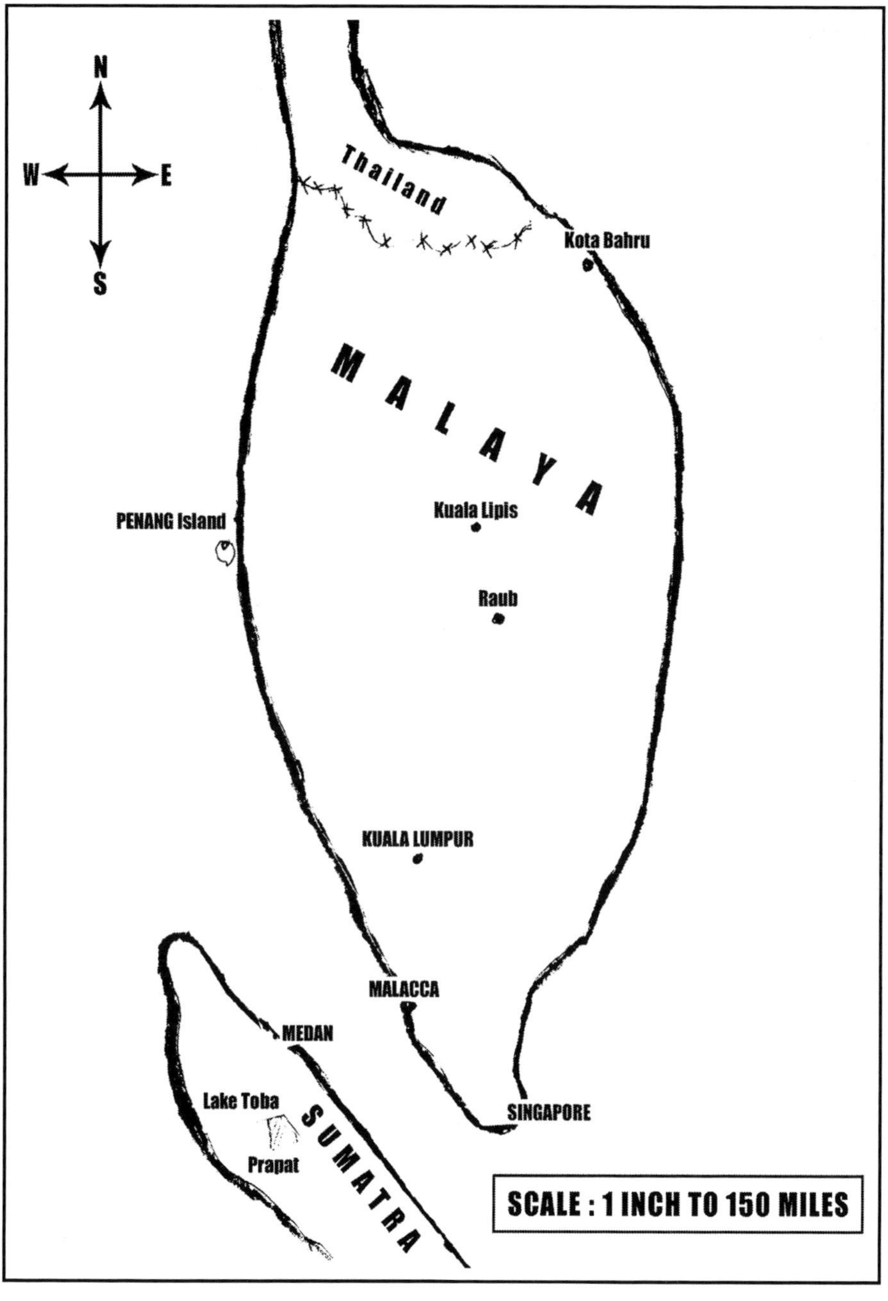

Map of Malaya

During the next three years I saw very little of them – I managed to get a ‘lift’ twice in a tiny little ‘Auster’ aeroplane used as a spotter plane by the artillery. I also used to be taken up in one of these planes now and again to view any area I might be operating in. Later on, back in the UK, I used these same spotter planes for my aerial photographic activities.

Going back to my Camp Commandant post, one day the Brigade Commander sent for me and said that a vacancy for a company commander had arisen in the 6th bn. stationed in Raub. I wasted no time in joining this bn., where I was given command of B Company, which was, at the time of my arrival, out on an operation in the jungle. However, I had decided that they must get to know me and my character as soon as possible so, when they arrived back in camp, weary and dirty, I drilled them up and down for ten minutes or so, then told them to go and get cleaned up before I had them reassembled in the dining tent. I then gave them a talk about my past, and plans for the future – saying, amongst other things, that I not only intended to achieve the highest score of CTs (Communist Terrorists) or sometimes called bandits – but also to achieve this without sustaining any casualties. Three years later when I left, the company had achieved both of these objectives.

Chapter 30 : 1953

Post-War Malayan Political Situation

Before going any further I will try to briefly describe the situation in Malaya after the war against Japan was over. In Malaya the population included a large proportion of Chinese, who were communist orientated and they looked to China for help etc. China would have liked to take over the Malayan peninsular after the British had gone. In the meanwhile we were very much there with a Governor General in residence, a civil service and police force officered by British officers and of course British Army troops to keep the peace. There was only one battalion of Malay soldiers with British officers. During the war the communist element of the Chinese community started an anti-Japanese underground movement in the country. This movement formed quite large groups, which lived in the jungle and committed various acts of sabotage against the Japs. Their leader was a man called Chin Peng and when the war was over he was decorated with an OBE for his support of the British rule. He was to become the greatest thorn in side of the government, as he and his movement, with Chinese backing, set about trying to undermine the British rule with the hope of taking over the country after our departure. He himself roamed around in the jungle all over the country but it was believed that he spent most of his time either in Thailand or on the border just inside Malaya – in the north. His movement was split up into groups of up to a hundred men – very often only in packets of thirty plus. However they had to have food, and they got this from collaborators who lived in the villages and were mostly workers of the rubber plantations. The rubber tappers would leave food etc. for these CTs at various prearranged points in the plantations. In order to prevent this 'leakage' the British Governor (Major Gen. Briggs, whom I served under for two years in the Western Desert campaigns) was instrumental in implementing what was to become known as the BRIGGS plan.

This policy forced all the rubber tappers to collect into villages, which were then surrounded by high barbed wire fencing from which they were not permitted to leave and each had a guardhouse at the entrance. The inhabitants were let out in the early morning, liable to be searched, and had to be back in the village by nightfall, after which they were not allowed to leave till the next morning. Not surprisingly, the Chinese were not happy with this – however they got used to it and did all they could to sneak things out to the CTs. As time went on these CTs had to find other ways of supplementing their diets and one of them was the clearing of small areas of jungle and planting crops. But these clearings had to be very small because large ones could be spotted very easily from the air and then ground forces would be sent in to destroy them and the CTs working on them. In the clearings they planted quick-growing cassava roots – not very nutritious but better than nothing I suppose.

Chapter 31 : 1953

Jungle Operations (1)

The primary job of the army in Malaya was searching the jungle with a view to eliminating all CTs, and therefore pre-empting the communist agenda for the country. By the time I arrived on the scene, the CTs in the jungle had suffered so many setbacks that they were reduced to operating, not in hundreds, nor fifties but in groups of three to five – mostly men of Chinese extraction, but there were some women CTs. Indeed, I took one girl (who had surrendered) out on an operation with me for some days. We went looking for a site where she had once lived and worked. My plan was to lie in wait around it and ambush any of her past companions who might return there. In the event no one turned up.

On another similar occasion, I went out with a captured CT who said he could take me to his last camp where his friends were hiding, so I set off to cross the Bera River and scoured the east bank but the camp had been vacated by the time we arrived. This man became very glum and told one of my men that he thought I would punish him for misleading information. The next evening I was lying in my hammock and heard a shot fired a few yards away from me. I found that this CT had put his rifle between his legs and shot himself through the forehead. Very inconvenient, as we had to lug his body back to base for three days. To carry these dead bodies we just tied their hands and ankles together and thrust a pole through them, we then had to have a man at each end to carry it.

On another occasion we had shot a CT and, as was the practice, I brought him back to the police station in a nearby township for identification purposes – It so happened that the police station was opposite to a local cinema outside of which a queue had formed for the 'next show'. Unbeknown to those in the queue the 'next show' was going to begin with the hog-tied CT! There was a great cry as the body was hoisted out of the truck and carried into the police station. The officer in charge told me there was nowhere to keep the body overnight. I pointed to a door and asked what was in there and he replied that it was a cell for prisoners, but at that moment it just housed a couple of drunks. I said, "Right, that will do" and left the corpse in the cell. I have often wondered what thoughts those prisoners had on waking the morning after!

As my life, for the next three years, was going to be very jungle orientated I will outline what this involved, as far I was concerned. I was in command of a company of Malay (Muslim) soldiers. The Company was divided into three platoons – each of about thirty men. I had one or two Malay officers and also, attached to me, was an Iban tracker from Borneo – a one-time head hunter who was quite a character and could shin up trees very easily. A great help when trying to retrieve our rations, which were dropped by parachute and then got tangled up in the branches 100 or more feet up in the overhead canopy. As a tracker, I don't think he was any better than I eventually became.

I would normally go out on operations with two platoons and leave the other behind at base, but this did depend on what the tasks were likely to be. I personally went out on nearly all of them. Usually these operations might take anything from one to two weeks and so we had to carry a lot of kit, weighing about 30 kilos. We took with us five-day rations, weapons and ammunition, water, and spare clothing to change into at night. It rained just about every day so one got soaking wet within the first hour, if not from the rain then from the wet foliage. Getting dressed in cold, wet clothes in the mornings was most unpleasant and I never really got used to it! Travelling through the jungle was no easy task either, as one could not walk upright, but had to bend, twist and turn to avoid the undergrowth and this took its toll. To cover 2 miles a day was average. To begin with I used to sleep on the ground and fix my groundsheet overhead but by this time I was an 'old man' of some 30 years and found the jungle not a comfy place to lie on so took the example of what the CTs would do and contrived a hammock. This involved getting a sheet of canvas (2 metres long and one metre wide) and making a fold at each end through which I would pass a short pole. Then, using parachute cord, I would tie these ends to a tree (there were plenty of them in the jungle!) and so I would have a flat canvas bed but, of course, this would swing so both ends had to be tied down, hard, to the base of the same trees.

Over this I would stretch my groundsheet to keep off the almost nightly rainstorms and underneath me, and my hammock, I would 'store' my weapon and dry clothing.

My method of searching the jungle for CT activity was as follows. We would set off in a specified direction. I would have two men in front of me and I would direct them from behind while the remaining 40 – 50 men would follow.

On reaching a point which I considered would be suitable for camp site, I would stop and indicate where my hammock would be erected and then, as a drill, the sections would fan out in a circle around my central point, and I would go round indicating their areas of responsibility. We would have 'stand to' every night and morning half an hour before sunset and half an hour before sunrise. I tried to get campsites alongside streams of rivers so that there was water for drinking, and ablutions.

If we heard anything, or saw any telltale tracks, I would stop to investigate. I would divide the men up into parties of four or five men under a responsible NCO and give each of these groups compass bearings fanning out from where I was waiting. They would search along these lines for about thirty minutes and then return to report to me. If nothing was found then we would advance a further 30 – 40 mins and repeat the procedure.

Every 5 days we were resupplied with rations etc. We would send a wireless message back setting out our requirements and give a rough estimate as to our whereabouts and the time to receive the airdrop. If possible we would select a clearing in the jungle then when the planes could be heard we would put up smoke signals and the planes would make their run in over us dropping the parachutes as close as possible to our signals. Of course, many times, the parachutes would get caught up in the 40-metre high trees and then we had to somehow get them down. I would use the Iban tracker attached to my company as he could shin up these trees without any difficulty. As a reward I would let him keep one of the parachutes. I personally did not ever call for a supply of any liquors in the airdrop. Another small rule I had was that everyone should be shaved. During the war we were very particular about this in the Indian Army, as an unshaven officer, I believe, sets a very bad example. I noticed that the SAS operating in Malaya did not follow this practice. They held the mistaken opinion that, being unshaven, one was then a tough guy.

One of my first operations was initiated by an aerial sighting of a clearing suspected as being a potential CT cultivation plot. I set off with a platoon to search this site and after a couple of days when we got near to where we were aiming for I went slowly ahead with just five men. After a while we heard the sound of wood being chopped and voices. I crept forward and saw three CTs in this small clearing. I called up three of the men with me and sent them round to the far side with instructions to kill at least one of them, the other CTs, I reckoned, would then almost certainly make a dash away from the direction the firing had come from i.e. towards me. And this is what one survivor did. He was carrying a shotgun. When he got to about 15 metres from where I was lying in wait with the Iban tracker I took aim and pulled the trigger but to my chagrin nothing happened – the CT was running away into the jungle but he had not seen me at that stage. I waved to the Iban to shoot but he just looked in my direction uncomprehendingly, so I got up and chased this CT pushing my way through the undergrowth. Just as I got near to him, he must have heard my approach, for he swung round with his gun – so I leaped through the air with my gun and crashed down on him, after which a wrestling march ensued but, being the bigger man, I soon got him in a headlock and held him like that. I then looked round to see what the Iban was doing, and saw his arm descending with his large parang obviously with a view to cutting off the head of the CT. With my free arm, I managed to stop the parang descending the full distance but even then, the man sustained a very nasty cut across the back of his neck. That episode over I went back to join my other men and was eventually able to call up (on my wireless set) a helicopter to take the CT back to hospital and captivity. The sequel to this capture was that the man recovered and some months later he was brought to trial. He now looked very fit and healthy and was charged with being in the jungle and armed – a capital offence. I was called as the main witness, he was found guilty and subsequently hanged and I was Mentioned-in-Despatches!

Chapter 32 : 1954

Jungle Operations (2)

I went on many such operations. A young English officer was sent to join my company. He was only 19 or 20 years old and serving his time in the National Army Service – compulsory in those far off days. Being new, certainly to jungle operations, I had to teach him everything I knew. So, to start with, I let him share a bivouac with me. Not for long though, as on these jungle ops one would sweat at lot and what with the humidity etc., the smell could be quite unpleasant so, by mutual agreement, we soon decided to part company – as far as the bivouac was concerned anyway!

Back in my base camp I got news of some CTs in a certain area so I sent him off with a platoon to investigate. After three days he got in touch with me on the wireless set in the evening, as was the custom, informing me that they had caught up with the CTs, had killed one and asked what he should do with the corpse. As he was more than three days' march away, and therefore too far to carry the body, I told him just to take a photo of the man's face for identification purposes but he replied that he had forgotten to take the camera with him when he set off. As this was normal procedure I, rather crossly, suggested that he cut the head off and gave the usual 'Roger and Out' to terminate the interchange. Three days later he arrived back and came to my tent where I was having dinner. He dropped a sandbag on the floor and from it rolled the CT's head! Out of curiosity I asked him whom he had got to carry out the amputation. He replied that he didn't feel like telling any of the men to do this somewhat distasteful task so he cut it off himself!

On still yet another occasion aerial observers reported a possible CT camp on the edge of a jungle lake. I was allotted three helicopters and told to go and investigate. We set off, but as there was no obvious landing place there was only one thing for it; and that was to climb down a knotted rope from the helicopter, drop into the lake and hope (a) it was not too deep and (b) that the bottom was firm and not boggy. When we got to the lake, I could see the camp so I went gingerly down the rope and even more gingerly into the water. I touched bottom after about one metre and was able to wade ashore, meanwhile waving the rest of my men to come and join me from their helicopters. This they did and, very fortunately, the CTs were no longer in residence, which was just as well as I would have been a sitting duck climbing down the rope and wading slowly ashore.

On some of my operations I had quite large commands consisting, sometimes, of companies from the Ghurkhas, The King's African Rifles, British regiments and detachments from the artillery regiments. I found the Malay soldiers very agreeable and always polite to a fault. I never ever had any trouble with them. When I left, the Malay Regiment (and the army) gave me a saddening send off and it gave me great pleasure to remind them of my initial speech and promise – no casualties whatsoever during my term of command. I was replaced by a Malay officer – a very nice chap who did not, I fear, stick to my rules of watchfulness and security and so, regrettably a month or so later I heard that the company had sustained a number of casualties by falling into an ambush – details of which I was not to know.

Chapter 33 : 1951 – 1954

Holidays While in Malaya

While serving in Malaya we had four holidays. The first was to Bangkok, the second to Prapat on Lake Toba (Sumatra), the third to Penang and the fourth to Malacca (on the West coast). All were eventful, with the usual traumas I always associate with holiday travel.

Bangkok

When we went to Bangkok it was in 1954, at that time it had not gained its present day notoriety as a holiday resort. In fact there were only two hotels of any standing and we booked into one of them. Tourism was well into the future. We left, to go by train, from Kuala Lumpur station. I had booked to stay the night, prior to our departure, at the Kuala Lumpur Station hotel. That night we went to the cinema – it had what we had never seen before, a wide screen. The film was Marilyn Monroe in *The River of no Return.* I had my wallet stolen from my back hip pocket during the performance and so, next morning, Sunday, I had to leave all sorts of instructions through the letter box of the Bank, which was closed and hope that they would send me money to the hotel in Bangkok as soon as possible.

It was very hot on the train with no air conditioning of course. We did however, have the compartment to ourselves. The journey took about two days, as I recall. Our hotel in Bangkok was quite comfortable – not luxurious, and was situated centrally. There are many many temples etc. to see and we went to see quite a few of them, but I was interested to learn that the town was a comparatively new one and nearly all the places of interest had been erected in the mid-19th century – though they looked much older. It has been called the 'Venice of the East' on account of the many canals. We could not do much as the money from Kuala Lumpur did not arrive until two days before we left. There were no such things as credit cards in those days.

Penang

This is a must (!) if you are ever in Malaya. We went by car and across to the island by ferry, so we were able to tour around and see the most important sights, including the snake temple, another temple with hundreds of tortoises etc. We had quite an experience on the way. I did not think that we would have any trouble getting a room for the one night in Taiping which was on our route. When we got there we could not get a room in any hotel, but were given an address that might be able to help us. The proprietor looked somewhat surprised to see us but showed us up to the first floor to a small room with one bed in it and the next door one as well. I took one and Greta & Felicity the other. In fact, the whole floor was just one large room partitioned off with thin walls, which finished 7 feet up. There were only a few lights up high near the ceiling and also a couple of fans and from these you got some light and air into your partitioned-off section. One also heard what was going on in all the other partitions – and there was plenty of that! In the morning it dawned on me that we had spent the night in a house of ill repute!

Prapat (Lake Toba, Sumatra)

In about 1954, (I'm not sure of my dates) I selected, literally by a random pinprick, a place in Sumatra. I could read one name on the small-scale map and that was what looked like a lake and town named Prapat on the edge of a lake. I wrote off a letter, in English, addressed to "The Manager, The Hotel, Prapat, Sumatra" and awaited a reply. To my surprise I got one saying that rooms had been booked as requested. To get there I went to a shipping company and asked if any boats were going to the main port – Medan and booked a couple of cabins on a cargo steamer that plied that journey – it only took five or six passengers. On the appointed day we set sail and arrived at Medan the next day. Getting through the port formalities was easy for us as we were given VIP treatment – why I don't know, because other passengers (mostly Dutch) from other ships were given a tough time and had to hang about for hours. Anyway, I then had to set about getting transport from Medan to this place called Prapat – some 100 miles away I seem to recall.

Sumatra had been a Dutch colony but they had been booted out and there was little law in the land. There was no railway link to Prapat so I looked around for a car but no one was willing to take the risk of driving through the territory reputed to be alive with roving bands of bandits and other evildoers. So we went to a hotel to think things over. Word had got around about our plans for onward travel and in the morning a taxi driver arrived and said he would take us – at a price. This was agreed and off we set – I, in some trepidation I may say, for I had not told Greta of the hazards that we might meet. In the event nothing happened and we arrived safely at Prapat to find it was a very nice hotel on the lakeside. Better still we were allocated a small chalet right on the 'beach' of the lakeside from where we could bathe etc. We were the only hotel guests! So we had the place to ourselves. I do recall that the Indonesian Government had laid down that all hotels had to serve at least one Indonesian meal a day. On the face of it, this didn't seem too bad but in fact, that meal was not at all pleasant as the obligatory rice served with it was always tepid and mushy.

We enjoyed the peace and quiet, or at least I did, for I was very tired from my jungle operations. Lake Toba claims to be one of the highest lakes in the world and about three or four miles long. In the middle is quite a large island (Samosir) which we were told we must see as the inhabitants were very primitive and lived in communal houses shaped like boats with high prows and very low front doors. We arranged for a boatman to take us and were very interested in the village and the surrounding countryside. The inhabitants lived mostly on fish caught in the lake. It was still untouched by tourism. The time came when we had to return so we had to renegotiate the taxi trip back to Medan.

After a couple days of waiting for our cargo boat to arrive we stayed in a hotel – where a couple of Dutch doctors were also waiting to return to Singapore on the same boat as we were sailing on.

Malacca (Malaya)

When my tour with the Malay Regiment came to an end, rather than returning to the UK by air, I asked for the equivalent fare money and decided to go back by luxury liner. I managed to get a 1st Class passage on the Dutch Liner the *Willem Ruys*. We were to sail from Singapore so took a leisurely trip in my car (a Humber Hawk, which I took back to England with me on the same boat). We stayed in Malacca for about ten days. It is a very pleasant state and almost entirely inhabited by Malays – or was in those mid-1950s years.

Chapter 34 : 1955

Return to the UK, Photographic Business

The sea journey back from Malaya was uneventful and relaxing for which I was very thankful as the three years I had spent on jungle operations had taken their toll and I had lost a lot of weight. I was glad of the peace and quiet of shipboard life. The fantastic menus and food soon helped me regain the lost weight. We only made two stops – one at Colombo and the other Naples where we went ashore and visited not only the ruins of Pompeii but also a cameo factory.

We arrived back at Southampton during a bitterly cold spell then went up to Oxford and stayed with my mother at 97 Lonsdale Road.

I now had to try and find a job. I wrote off to many employers of various organizations, but as I was now an 'old man' of 36 years of age with no commercial experience or training I did not even get to being interviewed.

Before I left to go to Malaya I had joined the Royal Photographic Society and they sent me their monthly magazines etc. When I got out there my interest in the subject increased. I bought myself an even better camera, developing and enlarging equipment and had various magazines delivered to wherever I was serving and these I devoured voraciously. I also set up a sort of dark room in my tent – although this could only be used during the hours of darkness and did not, of course, have running water but I persevered nevertheless and took thousands of photographs which I then developed and printed. All this activity stood me in good stead for when I came out of the jungle as I had this other absorbing interest, which took my mind off the proximity of the jungle and what it might contain! Other officers who did not have another interest would get a bit broody and did not last too long whereas I did my full time of three years.

With this photographic interest in mind I started to look around for something that might be connected and saw an advertisement selling a photographic/studio business in Farnborough, Hants. The original owner had made good living out of it during the war years; indeed he retired while still in his forties. The business consisted of three studios, in Aldershot, Farnham and Farnborough where the workrooms and office were situated.

In each studio were a table, chair, a camera, tripod and lights. A young girl would be the operator. The lights were fixed and all she had to do was sit the individuals down in the chair or the babies on the table, say, "Smile please" and click the shutter. At the end of the day I, or someone, would collect the exposed films, take them to the workshops for processing and developing. The finished prints would go back for the girl to sell. She would be paid £3 per month and they all seemed quite content with that. Of course in those days, young people would live with their parents. Sometimes, if the girls were confident they would go out and assist with weddings. On occasions I would do as many as five or six weddings on a Saturday afternoon. As time passed and people started to buy their own more sophisticated cameras the clientele dropped off and they no longer had need of this type of 'professional' photography so I closed two of the studios but rented a larger one in Farnham, where I personally up-marketed my portraiture and, I think, I made a good job of it – but not enough to make a good living.

I then struck out in providing aerial photographs of factories, large estates, stately homes and so forth. I based myself on a small private airfield (Blackbush) at Camberley, Surrey. I would hire planes for £5 per hour. They were recycled Army spotter planes that had been bought for £700 and then hired out to amateur pilots. These pilots were only too willing to fly me around the countryside as I was paying for the plane hire. These planes were ideal for my purpose. They had a single wing on top supported by a strut and they travelled at about 60 – 80mph. I flew in them while I was in Malaya.

Before setting off I would remove the offside door (where I would be sitting) and tie a rope round my waist and then around the seat back. When we came to the target area (I always did the navigation) I would indicate the target to the pilot and he would go down from our cruising height of about 600 metres to 200 metres. I would then step out, put one foot on the strut keeping the other inside the plane and from this awkward windy position would take the photographs. I never made more than one run-in as I was operating from an illegal height and did not want to draw undue attention to my activities!

Well, in the end I started to run out of places to photograph that were within economical range of Camberley so I sold my business, my seven cameras and all the negatives and then tried for something else!

In about 1964 I joined an Estate Agency on the fringes of London, at Worcester Park and Tolworth. Although I lasted for four years I did not really like this work as all the 'double-talk' and people backing out of contracts etc. upset me, so then I had a go as an insurance and mortgage broker. This was awful, and I started on my wanderings once again.

Chapter 35 : 1974

Becoming a Golf Club Secretary

I had not played golf for 25 years and went out once or twice to play on the 9-hole courses in the Epsom Race Course. This gave me the idea of becoming a Golf Club Secretary, and so I got in touch with the Secretary of Golf Club Secretaries' Association.

He suggested that I do an attachment to a Golf Club to see if I was suited to this sort of work. The Golf Club I went to was St George's Hill, at Weybridge. The Secretary and I got on well together but he just didn't want me around him all day long and consequently I spent most of my time playing golf! I stayed at St George's Hill for, say, a month and I then had to find a Golf Club that would take me on.

I was speaking to a married friend about these plans when his wife chimed in and commented, or rather asked what qualifications I had to take on such a job. My friend replied for me saying that I was very qualified having passed through the University of Life – which I personally think was an apt reply considering my past!

I realized that these applications and interviews could well run into months. I had to earn some money to see me through. I couldn't hope to get and hold down a job and at the same time go off to attend interviews as and as when they arose. So I had to be my own boss. What better way than to become a minicab driver. I registered with a firm operating out of Kingston-on-Thames.

This was a busy company – operating in and around London including the two main airports and I found it to be a very arduous way of making a living especially when you are over 50 years of age. I had a car phone fitted and in theory I was on the 8a.m. to 5p.m. shift. But it didn't work like that at all. If, during the rush hour, one was sent off on a trip to King's Cross station at 4p.m. this could well take two hours at that time and you would not get back until after 8p.m. sometimes – because, on the way back you would get a call diverting you to go and pick up someone elsewhere in London and bring them to Kingston or thereabouts. It was a very interesting job in many ways but one in which I put on 2 stone in weight as I just ate junk food as and when passing bakeries etc. I could write reams and reams about the various trips and passengers (nice and nasty) I collected and delivered. I was asked once or twice to change shift and do the 8p.m. – 8a.m. one. This really was rough stuff as the passengers were either to be picked up from pubs or being taken home from parties. Sometimes, "Control", would telephone me well before my shift began and ask me to be at one of the airports by 8am. I did this work until December 1973, by which time I had been appointed to a golf club (Mannings Heath Golf Club at Horsham), starting on 1 Jan. 1974. Before joining this club I had a month to while away the time. I handed in my car phone and said goodbye, but that was not the end. For the whole of that month of December the Control kept telephoning me and saying that they were so busy and would I help out. The Control office would fix the prices for me and tell me I could take the money – they did not care as long as their clients were happy and they were not letting any one down. These journeys took me on longish trips to the South Coast, Norwich, Kent etc. I recall one woman, who I drove to Norwich, gave me a tip of 25p but generally I found that the tips, each week, exceeded my earnings.

For quite a few years I had not been making much money and we had to tighten our belts in every direction. We did not go on any holidays for over 10 years. Social life was minimal and that was confined to the family. Not surprisingly, my wife, Greta used to get pretty fed up and proceeded to make a life away from home and so eventually I told her that our married life was at end and she could do what she liked. I bought myself a small maisonette in West Ewell, Surrey and she moved into a bedsit in Surbiton. We did not meet again until about eight years later by which time I had arranged our divorce – dated 18 October 1978.

One day in 1969, after my marriage break-up, I was working in my estate agency office in Tolworth when a lady (Margaret Wragg) came to enquire about houses in the area as she was thinking of moving up from her Brighton house in order to be nearer to a post to which she had been appointed at Kingston Polytechnic. To cut a long story short I was hooked and we continued seeing each other for many years. She had two children but her husband had left her for another woman some five or six years previously, so we were both in much the same boat! She became a regular visitor to Mannings Heath Golf Club and Horsham, where I had bought myself a small terraced house in order to be near to the Golf Club. In 1981, about 10 years after we had first met, we got married on Christmas Eve at the Espom Registry Office. It was a cold winter's day with the snow falling softly and everyone busying themselves with last minute Christmas shopping. Margaret's son and daughter with their respective girl and boyfriends acted as witnesses. When the Registrar entered the 'marriage' room she looked around questioningly at the four young ones expecting two to step forward – instead, she got us! The ceremony then proceeded with my faltering stroke-impaired speech.

I spent many happy years at the Golf Club at Mannings Heath near Horsham in Surrey. I would play golf almost every day of the week and sometimes twice – not surprisingly, my handicap came down from the 16 I started with to 4. I played so much golf that the members got me a telephone answering machine and presented me with new set of clubs, mine being very vintage – some even pre-war! After nearly five years at Mannings Heath I was offered the Secretaryship at the prestigious Worplesdon Golf Club near Woking, Surrey. Being a Secretary is not a bed of roses as a lot of people suppose. One can get on very well with 750 or so members. But if one or two on the committee take exception to anything you do then life becomes not worth the hassle. At Worplesdon, there was one committee member who had been a past captain, his father before him too and also an uncle. He was a millionaire and a past Walker Cup player. When he started to try and manipulate me I would not have it and suggested to him that he would not like it if I came up to his London office of cornbrokers and advised him on how best to run his business. This did not go down well. The Captain was becoming, and eventually did become, an absolute alcoholic and he was goaded into nit-picking on matters of no consequence, so I handed in my notice. It took over five months before my replacement arrived so it was October before I got away. When my replacement arrived I had to vacate the house provided by the club. My replacement lasted for about two or three months before he too objected to the interference perpetrated by certain committee members.

While I was waiting to step down I applied for the Secretaryship of the Zurich Golf Club in Switzerland and was accepted. The snag was, that one only spent the eight months' golfing season at Zurich and then, when the snows arrived, you were expected to leave the country until the season was back in again; admittedly the pay was good and all transport to and from England was paid for. The present incumbent was a retired army officer as well and had been there for 25 years. I telephoned him and asked him how he got on with all the German members and how he coped with the language problem. He said that was not his problem – but theirs, as he spoke and did everything in English! He must have been popular, as they then wanted another English Army officer to take over from him.

When I put this proposition to Margaret she was not overjoyed at the thought of these long breaks in our relationship – indeed I was issued with the ultimatum "Zurich or ME". And so it came to pass that I gave up my Zurich plans, packed my bags and went to live with her in Epsom. And so I began another phase in an already eventful life.

Chapter 36 : 1979

Onwards, Epsom, Ross-on-Wye

I left Worplesdon Golf Club in October 1979 and went to live with Margaret and her family in Epsom, 43 Christchurch Mount. A few weeks later, while lighting a garden rubbish bonfire, I decided to hurry up the process, got a can of petrol and threw it on. There was a big blowback and I was engulfed in flames. Not good at all. The flames on the top half of my body soon died down but my acrylic trousers were soaked in petrol and continued to burn on for quite a while. Finally the flames subsided and went out. However, I was left with severe burns on my calf muscle and admitted into Roehampton Hospital where skin was grafted onto the burn area. I felt very sorry for myself, but was appalled at the far more severe burns other patients in my ward had sustained. I shall always remember one man in particular. He was a farm labourer and had been towing a trailer full of straw behind his tractor. For some reason I can't remember, this trailer caught on fire and, fearful that the flames might ignite the nearby farm buildings, he jammed on the brakes thus bringing the blazing trailer of straw on top of himself. He escaped, but with 95% burns. He had been admitted about two weeks before me but he was still in an awful state – one never heard any sound from him, but as soon as he was able to get up, he kept on hobbling around the ward to try to help the rest of us – even though he was the most serious case by far. A truly wonderful man.

In April 1980 I suffered a stroke that left me pretty well speechless for some months. I took speech therapy lessons and improved slowly and was able to take up golf again at Cuddington Golf Club. In the meanwhile, with much help and understanding from Margaret, our relationship towards each other was further cemented – so much so that on Christmas Eve 1981 we were married in Epsom Registry Office. Owing to my poor speech I could not hope to get any reasonable job so decided to train as a china restorer – with a view to it becoming a paying hobby. Margaret and I applied for a china restoration course down in Somerset. It cost us £280 for 10 days plus a refresher weekend later. This was a fairly basic course on mending breaks, fillings etc. but nothing about airbrush work. On completion of the course I set about practising what I had learned. I did this by buying cartons full of junk chinaware at auctions, breaking the pieces and repairing them. I did this for about eight months and then used to take tables at Antique Fairs just to show the standard of my work.

I carried on doing this all around Surrey, so eventually people got to know me and the work started coming in. As I progressed, so more and more work arrived. In 1984 I suffered a heart attack and had to undergo open heart surgery – a double by-pass. Then in 1992 I suffered more heart trouble and had to have an emergency triple angioplasty operation. Also in 1992 we decided to up sticks and move to near Ross-on-Wye in Herefordshire – our new home was called "The Old Barn", a converted apple storage barn built, we believe, in about 1720 and converted in 1988. We settled into our new environment fairly quickly; I to the Ross-on-Wye Golf Club and Margaret to her many activities i.e. The Ross Walking Group, French classes, NADFAS, Art Appreciation Society, U3A (University of the Third Age) and The Horticultural Society. In 1994 I suffered another stroke which, like the previous one, mainly affected my speech. Through all this I still carried on with my china restoration, but in late 2000 I decided, at 80 years of age, I would call it a day. And so I retired to my golfing, gardening, computing and writing my memoirs. And also to watching how our children and their children are progressing.

The eldest, my daughter Felicity, had moved out to Greece in about 1971 to marry a Greek – this marriage failed, but she then married another Greek with whom she lives very contentedly and has two children herself, Maria and Tomotei. Her husband, Pandelis, is a surveyor and also an oceanographer, having his own successful business in Athens. Felicity, with a partner, Linda, has set up her own antiques retailing business, also in Athens. From small beginnings they are now thriving. They return to the UK every so often to attend antiques fairs and auctions and purchase fresh stock for their excellent shop. Tim graduated very well at Edinburgh University obtaining a first class degree in Environmental Studies and from there went on to Imperial College, London University to take his masters degree.

Margaret's two children, Stephen and Helen are also making great headway in their chosen professions. Stephen went out to France on his own some 20 years ago and there has built up a very sound business teaching English as a Foreign Language to the staff of many large French commercial concerns. He no longer teaches himself, but has a large pool of teaching staff who do the actual teaching while he takes care of the administration and, more importantly, making the contacts and contracts with his existing and potential clients. Unfortunately his marriage foundered, but he has two children, Marie and Ewan, who we enjoy having to stay in their holidays. He is an excellent father to them and has also taken a great interest in Helen's three boys.

Finally, Helen – who has always been involved in the world of the Arts, promoting artists, facilitating education initiatives and creating numerous community projects. Having been the Director of the Community Dance and Mime Foundation she went on to become Artistic Director of the Ross-on-Wye International Festival. From nothing, it became one of the leading festivals in the UK. She has recently changed focus to become a teacher of drama at Haberdashers Monmouth School for Girls. As a single parent she has raised three sons, James, Tom and Calum. The eldest, James, is Head of Wyedean House at Monmouth School, rows in the first eight and plays in three bands. Tom and Calum are strong all rounders in sport, the performing arts and academic study.

Margaret and I are very proud of all our grandchildren and the distinct signs they each show in being successful in their future lives.

And that brings me to the end of my saga.

Chapter 37

The Misfits

I have mentioned elsewhere in these memoirs, certain officers who just did not make it in these wartime years, though they may well have proved successful in other spheres. Under stress or even imagined stress it is difficult to understand what men's minds can or cannot stand up to. The medical professions, and experts far more qualified than I, are still trying to come up with answers to this recurring problem.

Dr Moran, who was Winston Churchill's medical advisor, wrote a book titled the *Anatomy of Courage* based on his wartime experiences in World Wars 1 and 2. He holds that courage is a diminishing resource i.e. a wasting asset.

Mark Twain goes even further and wrote, "Courage is the resistance to fear, mastery of fear – not the absence of fear". A man without fear may well not be a brave man, just fortunate in his make-up – and I class the Ghurkha soldier as a prime example of this. Brigadier 'Birdie' Smith who served with them with great distinction later wrote his book *Even the Brave Falter* to bear this theory out.

I will give some more instances that I personally came across – you must be the judge in each case of whether the individuals concerned were unfortunates unable to control their innermost thoughts. I will not give actual names, but use their Christian names in the interests of anonymity.

David was educated at a well-known Public School, went on to the Royal Military College, Sandhurst and then entered the Indian Army and the same regiment as I did. He was a large man and good at sports. He joined us in the Western Desert in about 1942/3 just after the break through at Alamein. On the run up in Tunisia, we began to have doubts as to his soundness under fire and the CO had him sent back to the Delta to some job at the Base Reinforcement Camp at Mena.

A year or so later, when we had arrived in Italy for the campaigns there, he was returned to us again. He was not at Cassino, but joined the bn. for the drive up the east coast of Italy. He was put in charge of the mortar platoon. Before our advance started he would tell us of the great plans he had, and how he would place his mortars as far forward as possible and then he himself would go even further forward and get into an advantageous position close to the enemy line, where he could watch their every move and call up fire from his mortars with his wireless. We listened to all this and looked at each other in some wonderment. Came the day when we advanced towards the enemy lines, there was no sign of David. He had set his mortars down in a safe area well back and stayed there with them – he didn't go up to any of the forward companies to even look at the terrain from a distance. Once again, he was returned to base and I think that he went back to India where he obviously took stock of himself and decided off his own bat that he was no longer fit to be an officer. He resigned his commission and re-enlisted in the British Army as a private. What happened to him after that, I never heard.

Chris was the son of a school headmaster and was a quiet, well-read man. He came to us in the Western Desert in 1941 where we were in the 'Bagush Box' waiting to execute Auchinlech's push to the Omars and beyond.

He did not create a good impression, likeable though he was. He definitely gave out an atmosphere of some instability and so was sent back to our base outside Cairo. Two years later when we were advancing up through Tunisia he arrived back with us and was put in charge of the signal platoon. As I have said earlier we took up a position in the olive groves north-west of Enfidaville. Soon after arrival, the enemy decided to shell us. We had not sufficient time to dig very deep slit trenches and I was kneeling in mine when I saw Chris walking amongst the olive trees. I saw a shell drop near him and he was obviously wounded but he managed to crawl to a nearby trench where he took shelter. When the shelling stopped the stretcher bearers came and took him away and he was evacuated to hospital. A year or so passed and then we were in Italy where he rejoined us. As I said, he did not give the impression of an officer with much drive and so once again he was left behind while the bn. went up to Cassino.

Our Italian base camp was near a town called Caserta, I think, and nearby was an army hospital. Chris had time to make the acquaintance of one of the nurses, and unknown to her, he fell in love. One day he declared his love for her and asked her to marry him. Hardly knowing the man, it was not surprising that she turned him down. He was so upset that he went out into a field somewhere, lit a small fire and heated up a piece of metal. When it was red hot he proceeded to burn a heart and an arrow, plus her name onto his forearm – hardly the action of a coward! Anyway, he was sent back to India where we heard that he finished up in a mental asylum. But that is not the end of the story.

After I had completed the Staff College course in Quetta, I was posted down to Madras as GSO II (a staff appointment on brigade HQ) there. This was in 1946. One day the Commissioner of Police rang and asked me if I knew a chap called Chris. I had forgotten all about him, so was very surprised to hear of him again. It appears that Chris was found living very rough, in the native downtown district; he was inebriated, penniless and confused. I went to the police station where he was being held, took him out, got him washed and gave him a meal and arranged temporary accommodation until I could find something to do with him. In our conversation it came out that his father was still alive and school mastering up in the Punjab. I arranged a train passage for him, put him on the train and off he went. That was my good deed for the day, and I imagined that I would not hear from, or about him, again. (I never asked him and he did not tell me how he came to know I was holding that post in Madras!).

Many, many years passed – in fact nearly twenty years. In England in the 1960s there was a television programme presided over by Ludovic Kennedy. Four people would be asked some pretty erudite questions and at the end of the session one would go forward to the next round. There would be quarter, and semi-finals, culminating in the winner being declared Mastermind of Great Britain 1960, 1961, 62, 63 and so on. Chris gained this distinction for the year he entered it. As Margaret Thatcher, one day, would say, "It's a funny old world"!

Peter? I have forgotten his name after all these years. He was posted to our bn. also in the desert in 1941. It soon became very evident that although he was well educated, he was quite out of his depth as a regimental officer – I can't remember the many odd things he did, but one sticks in my mind: life in the Western Desert was made very miserable thanks to the literally millions of flies that tormented the army. In desperation for trying to find something for Peter to do the CO nominated him as 'Officer in Charge of Getting Rid of Flies'.

Later on this first day I happened to go into the officers' mess tent and to my surprise found him sitting there with a fly swatter in his hand. I asked what he was doing, to which he replied; he was getting rid of the flies! He honestly thought that was his sole occupation. It was the practice in those days, and perhaps it is now, that when adverse reports are made regarding an officer, he was given the right to see and comment on it. Our CO wrote such a report concerning him and asked to have him removed from the regiment. Such action had to be confirmed by a senior officer – in this case the corp commander. I was detailed off to escort Peter to the corp commander's HQ many miles away and on the way we had a long talk. There was nothing objectionable about him and we were on pretty friendly terms. I read his reply to the CO's report and it made very good reading, so I was very curious as to what the corp commander would make of it, because no specific charge had been laid against him. The result was that he was taken away from the regiment and posted to a British Regiment. Actually, I think that he should have been transferred to some sort of desk job such as Public Relations, publications, propaganda etc.

My parents, who were in India, used to send me magazines, newspapers and so forth. One day, while reading one of these, some two years later, I read the casualty listing from the Burma front and saw his name as having been killed in action.

Finally, we come to **Derek**. I knew him before I took command of a company in Malaya. He was, I think, a good active service soldier, but he had a problem, in that he thought he was tougher than he really was, and further more he drank more than his constitution could absorb, thereby setting a bad example to his soldiers. The exact reasons why he was sent away from his bn., I was not informed of, but probably related to those I have just outlined. He was sent to join my company, and I was instructed to keep an eye on him and, in due course, to report on his fitness to be an officer. He was about the same age as myself and we appeared to get on well together, but I told him straight that he was under review.

I sent him out on patrols and he did well, but I got one or two negative reports about his behaviour: that he would take liquor out with him, and obviously drank too much, that he became slovenly in his attire and had an unshaven appearance. I warned him to watch it, but he did not heed my warning. Eventually, one day, in my officers' mess tent he became obstreperous and when I reprimanded him he threw an accusation at me saying that I did not like him drinking, because I couldn't drink as much as him. I knew my capacity was far greater than his had ever been. I told the other officers to leave the tent, then I sent for bottles of whisky, which I placed before us, and we proceeded to drink for drink. This did not last very long, for he slid under the table and I escorted him to his tent.

The next day, I submitted my report and he was sent off to our depot at Port Dickson and there dismissed from the service. He was not a bad man – just too keen to prove his toughness and he considered himself a person who looked for war. He soon left Malaya. At that time (1955) there was a sort of civil war going on in Kenya with the Mau Mau tribe of that country causing trouble to the British administration. He went out there, presumably to re-enlist in the army or join the police in the hope of seeing more action. Whether he succeeded I don't know, but I do know that soon after his arrival in Kenya he was killed in an air crash.

Epilogue

After I came back to the UK in 1955, and my wanderings seemed to have come to an end, I have been asked by many people if I didn't find life very mundane in comparison to my past activities. I suppose it had become so, but I do not think of it in this way, and just press on with life as it comes along. I think, in retrospect, that my childhood and adolescent years probably left their mark on me. I was not brought up by my parents – in fact I learned to do without them. I had very little to do with the female sex – what with being at a boys' only boarding public school between the ages of 11 and 19 (the school is now co-educational!) and following this with four years in the Western Desert and later, three years in the Malayan jungles.

I became a smoker from the age of 21 and a very heavy smoker indeed, rising to well over a hundred cigarettes a day. From the age of about 22 my consumption of alcohol increased month by month – no doubt the war had something to do with this! I would say that for some four or five years, I consumed the equivalent of at least one bottle of spirits (gin, whisky) each day and on many occasions a good deal more – but all this time, I was living mostly out of doors in the fresh air and taking a lot of exercise. I can only remember one occasion in all this time when I was not in full possession of my faculties and that one occasion was in private, when no one else was around – so I don't consider myself ever to have been an alcoholic. I gave up smoking when I was 40 years of age. I had no difficulty doing this once I had made up my mind – I just stopped.

Looking back on my life, I think that I could say that I was a good soldier, a good District Officer, a poor Government civil servant, a good photographer, a poor estate agent and insurance broker, a good minicab driver, a good golf club secretary and a good china restorer. But, overall, if success in life is judged by material wealth – and it is in this very material world in which we now live, then I cannot, as an almost professional rolling stone, claim to have gathered much moss – so I suppose that I too must fall into the category of being a 'misfit'!

Appendix A

A Few Facts and Figures About the 4th Indian Division

I quote from Field Marshall, Lord Wavell. C-in-C the Middle East Forces, General Officer Commanding India and later Viceroy of India:

> *"Those who have fought under the sign of the RED EAGLE will always be justly proud of it and those commanders who have known the worth in the field of that magnificent division will be the first to acknowledge their debt of gratitude, and to salute one of the greatest bands of fighting men who have ever served together in this troubled world of wars and warriors. The fame of this division will surely go down as one of the greatest fighting formations in military history: to be spoken of with such as Caesar's 10th Legion, Wellington's Light Division of the Peninsular War, and Napoleon's Old Guard."*

The 4th Indian Division was first formed in 1940 in Egypt. Over the years the units were changed owing to their long active service, or their heavy casualties.

An infantry division consists of:

Division HQ – A regiment of Artillery – Royal Engineers – RAMC – RAOC – RASC, An Anti-craft regiment – A Cavalry Regiment – A Machine bn. – Royal Signals and Three Infantry Brigades each comprising of three battalions. In this division these brigades were each made of 1 British bn. – 1 Indian bn. – 1 Ghurkha Bn. The artillery were British; the cavalry were Indian; the REs (Sappers and Miners) were Indian; (The RAMC had both British and Indians doctors and orderlies). The RASC and RAOC likewise had both

> British and Indian ranks. An average division would have a total strength of around 12,000 men. It will be seen that although this was called an Indian Division it was, in fact, about 60% Indian troops and 40% British. Over the whole period of the war, although the units did change, the spirit of the Division seemed to transfer itself from unit to unit as the newcomers came in. There is one thing worth mentioning and that was the great comradeship between the British and Indian soldiers – no colour bar. There were many instances of British soldiers supporting their Indian friends if there was ever any form of insult directed against the Indians who were too polite to retaliate.

The division (sometimes called the 'Red Eagle' Division because of its insignia, worn on the shoulder and painted on all vehicles), travelled more than 15,000 miles, suffered more than 25,000 casualties, and captured over 150,000 prisoners. Its campaigns included Eritrea, Western Desert (3 campaigns) Syria, retreat from Benghazi, Libya, Tunisia, and in Italy – Monte Cassino and the breaching of the Gothic Line, then too there was Greece – trying to prevent a civil war and the communist party from taking over the country. And last, but not least, trying to keep the peace in the horrendous massacres and lawlessness resulting from the partition of Pakistan and India in August 1947.

The Honours and Awards the division earned were very considerable and these are set out below:

VC	Victoria Cross	**4**	
DSO	Distinguished Service Order	**67**	*Officers*
GC	George Cross	**4**	
GM	George Medal	**2**	
MC	Military Cross	**205**	*British Officers*
KBE	Knight Commander of British Empire	**1**	
CBE	Commander of British Empire	**7**	
OBE	Order of the British Empire	**11**	
MBE	Member of the British Empire	**8**	
MM	Military Medal	**132**	*British Other Ranks*

DCM	Distinguished Conduct Medal	**27**	*British Other Ranks*
IDSM	Indian Distinguished Service Medal	**244**	*Indian all ranks*
IOM	Indian Order of Merit	**115**	*Indian VCOs and Ors*

Mentioned-in-Dispatches	**665**
And numerous foreign awards	
e.g. Croix de Guerre (French)	**11**
American Bronze Medal	**4**

The Division also has the distinction, I believe, of being the only one to have its own memorial chapel. This is located in the Chapel of the Royal Military Academy, at Sandhurst. The crests of all the battalions and other units, which served in the division, are affixed around this side chapel. The division is also the only one that has its own large brass candlesticks standing proudly on each side of the altar.

Every year, after a Sunday communion service at Sandhurst, the 4th Indian Division Officers' Association held a short service of remembrance in this side chapel, at the termination of which a bugler plays *The Last Post* and we all follow this intoning the Division's motto – in Urdu: "JO HUKM" ("That which is ordered will be done)". I attended nearly every service since it was inaugurated but, sadly, with the passing of the years our numbers became so depleted that the Reunion finally gave up in 2003.

Appendix A

Below is a copy of our Menu at the 1964 dinner when our various senior commanders were remembered in the names of the various courses.

4th Indian Division Officers' Association

MENU

Le Saumon Fumé Maréchal Wavell

Le Consommé Marmite Maréchal Wilson

Le Dindonneau Rôti Maréchal Auchinleck
Les Boutonnettes Maréchal Alexander
Les Pommes Maréchal Montgomery

La Cassata Général O'Connor

La Croûte Général Godwin-Austen

Le Café Général Freyberg

United Service Club **24th October, 1964**

Appendix B

The Closing Years of Some Empires

Approximate Dates of Independence of Various Countries From Their Rulers (the dates cannot always be definate as the process could, and did, spread over years).

The author happened to have served (in various capacities) in all but two of these countries from 1942 to 1979.

1942	Egypt / Sudan	*(from Great Britain)*
1942	Libya	*(from Italy)*
1943	Tunisia	*(from France)*
1945	Syria	*(from France)*
1946	Palestine / Jordan	*(from Great Britain)*
1947	India / Pakistan / Bangladesh	*(from Great Britain)*
1948	Burma	*(from Great Britain)*
1954	French Indo-China	*(from France)*
1957	Malaysian Federation	*(from Great Britain)*
1959	Cyprus	*(from Great Britain)*
1961	Tanganyika	*(from Great Britain)*
1965	Singapore	*(from Great Britain)*
1979	Zimbabwe / Zambia / Malawi	*(from Great Britain)*

Ronald Perkin

Photo taken in Quetta (1945)